THE
COSMIC
BREATH

THE
COSMIC
BREATH

Reclaim Your True Flow: Breathing Through Trauma, Embracing Cosmic Love

Donna Evans Strauss

1 2 3 4 5 6 7 8 9 0

ISBN #978-1-965512-01-2

Dedication

To the wisdom keepers of our ancestral heritage, whose timeless teachings on the breath remind us of life's essence. From the sages of yoga, like Patanjali, to the masters of Qigong, and the prophets and mystics of biblical traditions—your eternal wisdom unites and directs us toward the sacred rhythm of the cosmos.

To the modern visionaries of conscious breathing, who have dedicated their lives to exploring enlightened embodiment: Wilhelm Reich, Alexander Lowen, John Pierrakos, Barbara Brennan, and so many others—your bravery and commitment inspire us to embrace the profound power of our breath, leading us toward wholeness and presence.

May this work honor your legacy, nurturing the journey of reconnecting with the breath—the bridge between spirit and body, and the gateway to our infinite potential.

Table of Contents

Introduction

Breath is the bridge that connects life to consciousness, which unites your body with your thoughts. Whenever your mind becomes scattered, use your breath as the means to take hold of your mind again. –Thich Nhat Hanh

Many often take breathing for granted, yet it is key to unlocking a deeper connection to the cosmos and your inner self. Why not, it is autonomic and doesn't require moment to moment attention. It pulsates and underlies the very core of our physical existence and provides the cosmic life force that activates every system and cell of our body. It wasn't until studying trauma and health within the body that I discovered that breath is essential to revitalizing and reclaiming our true nature. We are reminded in Genesis, where God formed Adam by "breathing into his nostrils the breath of Life."

This act illuminates that the cosmos, God, the Infinite Intelligent Universe, initiates our descent into human form. In *The Cosmic Breath*, we reclaim our true nature and flow while releasing traumas or restrictions. Love is our essential nature and emerges from the depths of our being. In the pages of this book, you will uncover the greater mystery of how your breath and breathing patterns can unlock your true potential for health, love, and happiness.

Did you know that the normal respiratory rate of a person ranges from 12 to 20 breaths per minute, which adds up to around 17,000–30,000 breaths per day (American Lung Association, 2017)? These numbers are easier to appreciate when you know what happens when breathing stops. When you stop breathing, your body goes through a series of critical events, all within a little over 10 minutes. As carbon dioxide levels in your blood rise and oxygen levels drop, you experience respiratory acidosis. Within two minutes, your brain starts suffering from oxygen deprivation, causing neurons to malfunction and leading to loss of consciousness. After four minutes, permanent brain damage can occur, and after ten minutes, severe brain damage is almost inevitable (Spinalcord.com Team, 2021). Beyond that, the chances of survival drop dramatically, and even if you're resuscitated, irreversible brain damage is highly likely. If breathing isn't restored at this point, death usually follows.

In the Buddha at the Gas Pump interview transcript, Jude Currivan, Ph.D. a cosmologist, and author of *The Cosmic Hologram* and *The Story of Gaia* refers to the universe's inception as the "Big Breath" rather than the "Big Bang," Her theories suggest the fabric of the universe consist of in-formation that expands consciousness, a holographic reality, by highlighting its fine-tuned and ordered nature. Breath, a quintessential life force, transmits highly sophisticated in-formation as frequency sequencing that interacts and activates the code held within all life (https://batgap.com/jude-currivan-transcript).

This makes us question our knowledge regarding breath. What if our breaths are reflections of a larger, universal process? Could the expansion and contraction of the cosmos be echoed in the rise and fall of our breathing? What if the way we breathe could cause harm to our body? And what if I told you there are breath techniques that can also bring physical, mental, and emotional healing? In *The Cosmic Breath*, you'll learn all this and more. This book is a journey into the world of breathwork, where ancient wisdom blends with modern insights to show how something as overlooked as breathing can lead to incredible personal transformation.

In over 35 years of experience, I have worked with thousands of students, clients, and groups, following the life pulse and wave of breath to identify trauma and release faulty assumptions about life. One remarkable case involved a 78-year-old man diagnosed with stomach cancer, which was believed to be caused by asbestos poisoning from his auto mechanic business. During our session, I noticed he repeatedly said, "I can't stomach it." When I asked him to breathe into his stomach and repeat this phrase, he recalled a traumatic experience from his youth. At 16, he and his father were in a concentration camp, where the air smelled of death, and they were terrified and distraught. His father's death in the camp had left my client with deep-seated emotions that he buried in his stomach. We then began to release the trauma held deep within his body, all by following his breath and addressing these suppressed feelings.

This procedure wasn't magical; it was based on healing knowledge that has existed since the beginning of time but that many practitioners have forgotten about or overlooked. These techniques are based on cosmic wisdom that recognizes the power of breath to unlock and release deeply held emotional and physical blockages in our bodies.

In this guide, we'll explore age-old practices that have stood the test of time to reveal the spiritual and historical roots that shape our understanding of breath. We'll combine ancient teachings with modern science to demonstrate how breath and universal energy are interconnected and how the quality of your breath reflects your overall health. Additionally, we'll share practical techniques and concepts that you can apply in your daily life to release trauma, anxiety, fear, and PTSD through effective breathing techniques.

You'll discover valuable advice and practical exercises suitable for your journey, whether you're new to breathwork or have been practicing for years. This guide is an invitation to experience the life-changing power of conscious breathing.

Mindfully written to address your most pressing issues about breath through a combination of practical advice, scientific explanations, and spiritual reflections, *The Cosmic Breath* will pave your path to inner peace and healing.

Are you excited to embark on this life-changing adventure? Take a breath, hold it, let it out, and let's begin!

Chapter 1:

Principles of Cosmic Breath

He lives most life whoever breathes most air.
–Elizabeth Barrett Browning

Breathing is far more than a simple biological function; it serves as a profound bridge between the physical body and the vast, interconnected energy of the cosmos. This chapter introduces the concept of cosmic breathing, delving into its meaning and essence while exploring its spiritual and scientific significance. We'll uncover how the act of breathing not only sustains life but also serves as a gateway to higher awareness, connecting us to the universal flow of energy that surrounds and permeates everything.

In addition to the theoretical foundation, this chapter offers practical guidance on incorporating cosmic breathing into your daily life, empowering you to harness its transformative potential. By the time you finish this chapter, you'll gain a deeper understanding of the breath's incredible power and how it can enhance your physical vitality, spiritual awareness, and emotional balance.

The Essence of Cosmic Breath

Cosmic breath extends beyond the air you breathe in and out; it is the breath of life in everyone and everything, including the universe. While normal breathing is a physiological process, cosmic breathing includes the spiritual and energetic aspects of breathing. It is an intentional and purposeful way of breathing that helps you align with the universe to draw energy and knowledge from a higher power. Cosmic breath practices assist in balancing your internal energy, which aids in increasing consciousness, engaging in deeper meditation, and achieving a better connection with the environment. Understanding the true nature of cosmic breath and how it can positively change your life requires a comprehensive understanding.

The history of cosmic breath can be traced back in time to different ancient civilizations that, in one way or another, improved the knowledge and practice of breathwork. The practice of breath control, also known as pranayama, is recorded in the ancient Indian literature of the Veda, particularly within the Upanishads, which are some of the oldest sacred scriptures (Phillips, 2009). These texts describe the breath as a means of reaching other levels of awareness and spirituality. Pranayama is part of yoga and meditation, and it involves specific exercises aimed at regulating the breath and controlling prana, or life force. Life force flows through all living beings, and its regulation through pranayama practices is believed to purify the mind and body, improving spiritual growth (Ahuja, 2023).

Breathwork has different meanings in different cultures in different parts of the world; each has its own perspective. The Indigenous people of different cultures around the world believe that breath is the soul that links us to the Earth and the universe. For example, in Native American culture, breathwork is incorporated into rituals and ceremonies to heal diseases, foster spiritual development, and facilitate communication with ancestors.

In Eastern cultures, breath is considered the life force and the way to spiritual awakening. Aikido, practiced in Japan, involves using breathing patterns to coordinate the physical movements of the body with the mind and the universal energy referred to as ki (Ohnishi & Ohnishi, 2006). Similarly, the practice of breath control is used in Tibetan Buddhist meditation techniques to reach a state of heightened awareness and spiritual enlightenment.

Breath is also a significant aspect of some African traditions as a means of communicating with divine powers. It is used in many African spiritual practices, where it is believed to contain a life force and is utilized to call upon the spirit of protection. In ancient Egyptian culture, breath was considered sacred and linked to the soul. The word ka in ancient Egyptian refers to the life force that follows a person throughout their life and into the afterlife (Davies, 2018). Proper breathing was considered critical for maintaining one's ka; this ensured health and spiritual protection.

Science, psychology, and New Age spirituality have widely accepted breathwork, making people across different cultures appreciate and embrace it as a way of life. Scientific studies show that the rate and depth of your breathing can impact your autonomic nervous system by influencing stress and relaxation. The autonomic nervous system is a component of the peripheral nervous system, which helps manage involuntary processes such as regulating blood pressure, controlling the heart rate, and maintaining smooth muscle functions such as digestion (Russo et al., 2017).

Research also shows that methods such as diaphragmatic breathing and alternate nostril breathing help decrease levels of cortisol, a hormone that increases in the body during stressful times. This practice also improves heart rate variability and emotional regulation (Ma et al., 2017). Modern medicine has recognized breathwork and incorporated it into the treatment of people with anxiety, depression, and PTSD. Moreover, modern psychology has fields such as bioenergetics and somatic experiencing, which also apply breathwork to free your body from accumulated trauma.

Contemporary spirituality utilizes breathwork as one of the ways to help people transform their lives. Techniques such as holotropic breathwork involve the use of intense breathing patterns that cause an altered state of consciousness and aid in spiritual and emotional metamorphosis. Additionally, practices such as rebirthing breathwork and transformational breathing have become popular because they allow individuals to connect with their inner selves and let go of any negative subconscious thoughts.

Unlike ancient practices, which might have been confined to specific cultural or religious contexts, modern breathwork is accessible to anyone seeking to improve their quality of life. This democratization of breathwork has made it popular, and many people from different parts of the world are now practicing breathwork and testifying to the changes it has brought in their lives.

Jude Currivan's Cosmic Hologram

Jude Currivan, famous for her efforts in integrating science and metaphysics, introduced the concept of the cosmic hologram, which captures the universe as a single holographic structure. In the cosmic hologram, every minuscule part of the universe holds information about the entire cosmos, mirroring how each fragment of a holographic image depicts the whole.

Jude Currivan's theory from her book *The Cosmic Hologram* introduces a fascinating concept, suggesting that the universe may not have started with a big bang but with a big cosmic breath. Instead of beginning with an explosive event, the universe could be expanding and contracting simultaneously, similar to the process of breathing (Currivan, 2017).

This theory suggests that just like we breathe, the universe breathes too, and these breaths determine the evolution of the universe and our position in it. We can relate this point of view to concepts from ancient times that considered the universe to be alive. In some sense, we still consider the universe to be alive; the terms father time and mother nature personify the universe to this end. Interpreting the universe as a cosmic breath corresponds to many religious concepts that teach the unity of all existence and the importance of breath as vital energy flowing through all organisms. Incorporating the findings of Currivan's work into the knowledge of breathwork helps improve your relationship with the universe and, therefore, your quality of life.

Spiritual Significance of Cosmic Breath

In the spiritual world, breath is fundamental in most holy scriptures, where it is described as the beginning of life. The idea of breath as life is found in many religions and cultures. In the Bible, the book of Genesis 2:7 tells us, "'And the Lord God formed man of the dust of the ground, and breathed into his nostrils the breath of life; and man became a living soul'" (The Holy Bible, New King James Version, 1982). This demonstrates that God gives us the gift of life, which is breath. In the same way, Acts 17:28 says, "For in Him we live, and move, and have our being" (The Holy Bible, New King James Version, 1982). This verse also points to the fact that existence is a continuous flow of divine breath from the Creator.

In Islamic culture, the Quran describes how Allah blew life into creation. Thus, Surah Sad verse 38:72 says, "So when I have fashioned him and had a spirit of My Own 'creation' breathed into him, fall down in prostration to him" (The Noble Quran, 1997/n.d.). This verse also indicates that the breath of Allah is what gives life and spirit to humans.

In Hinduism, prana, or vital energy, is the breath of Brahman, or the supreme absolute reality. This life energy is present in every living organism; through activities like pranayama, one can learn to regulate and increase this energy, which results in spiritual enlightenment and realization of the self.

As the renowned astrophysicist Neil deGrasse Tyson, once explained, the very air we breathe connects us to every living being that has ever walked the Earth. In his words:

"They're more molecules of air in every breath you take than there are breaths of air in all the atmosphere of the earth. So when you exhale, there's enough of those molecules to scatter into every breath of air that is inhaled. So when you take a breath of air, you have molecules of air that went through the lungs of Jesus" (2024).

The oxygen molecules you draw into your lungs may have been exhaled by ancient philosophers, powerful kings, or even Jesus himself. Our atmosphere is a closed system, endlessly recycling the same molecules over millennia. With each breath, we unknowingly participate in a cosmic dance, inhaling the stories of the past and exhaling the seeds of the future. This realization reveals how intimately we are tied to history and to each other. Every breath binds us not only to those who came before but to those who will one day follow.

Connection to the Divine

Let us explore further how various religions connect breath with divine power. The Bible teaches that "All Scripture is God-breathed and is useful for teaching, rebuking, correcting, and training in righteousness, so that the servant of God may be thoroughly equipped for every good work" (The Holy Bible, New King James Version, 1982, 2 Timothy 3:16–17). This suggests that the breath embodies divine inspiration and guidance, emphasizing our link to the wisdom and power of the Divine.

In Buddhism, breath meditation, also called anapanasati, is a fundamental practice that centers on mindful breathing to cultivate inner peace, improve concentration, and boost spiritual insight, leading to a profound state of meditation. The practice serves as a gateway to profound inner transformation by anchoring awareness to the rhythm of the breath. The practitioners cultivate a deep clarity of spirit and understanding of the cosmic potential that is within every person.

Sufism, a branch of Islam, emphasizes the importance of breath in spiritual practices. Sufi breathing techniques, like Hosh dar Dam (awareness in breathing), promote mindfulness and improve one's relationship with God. These practices aim to purify the soul and attain theosis. Through the deliberate focus on each inhale and exhale, Sufis believe the breath becomes a conduit for divine presence, a sacred rhythm that aligns the soul with the eternal. Hosh dar Dam teaches that every breath is an opportunity to remember God, transforming the simple act of breathing into a profound connecting spiritual act (Naqshbandi Principle, 2014). As the breath flows, so does the seeker's awareness of the divine, creating a union between the finite self and the infinite. Sufi mystics often describe this practice as a way to cleanse the heart, quiet the ego, and draw closer to God's essence. In the silence between breaths, you may hear the whispers of the divine, a reminder that the breath is not merely life-sustaining—it is life-affirming.

In the Jewish tradition, the Hebrew word for breath, ruach, is also synonymous with spirit. Breath is seen as a manifestation of God's spirit within us, a constant reminder of our divine origin and connection to the Creator. These religions acknowledge breath as a meaningful spiritual practice that serves to connect us with the Divine, leading to peace of mind and enlightenment. Participating in activities consistent with the universal life force helps you strengthen your general well-being and deepen your spiritual relationship.

Cosmic Energy Flow

You can think of cosmic energy flow as the energy that moves through your body, mind, and spirit while connecting you to the universe and all living beings. In *Hands of Light*, Barbara Brennan describes this energy as a field surrounding your body like an invisible bubble, known as the aura. This field connects to different layers of your body, mind, emotions, and spirit (Brennan, 1990). Those who have received training in the art of energy healing can see and manipulate this field. The control of this field can help achieve physical, emotional, mental, and spiritual healing.

Cosmic energy flow goes beyond your surroundings; it also allows you to connect with other living organisms and outer space. This link serves to show the interconnectedness of all things. This energy force moves through our bodies on special channels called meridians. These pathways help transport energy easily. The obstruction of this flow can make you feel spiritually disconnected or out of sync with the world.

Different spiritual traditions believe that learning to work with the cosmic flow is part of spiritual growth. This energy flow helps you meditate, trust your instincts, and feel connected to everything.

Integrating Science and Spirituality

Science helps us improve our understanding of why breathwork is so powerful for our body and mind. By systematically looking at breathing from different scientific angles, which include biology, physics, and quantum mechanics, we can bridge the gap between ancient practices and modern scientific knowledge.

When we think of fundamental biological processes in the human body, breathing is often one of the first that come to mind. The act of inhaling air in and out of the lungs aids in delivering oxygen and exhaling carbon dioxide, which is a waste product. Breathing facilitates the chemical process of respiration, the process by which cells use oxygen to break down glucose to produce energy. This energy is essential for all cellular functions and human survival. Without proper respiration, cells are not able to function properly, ultimately leading to organ failure and, if prolonged, mortality.

On a molecular level, oxygen enters the alveoli in the lungs and diffuses into the bloodstream, where it binds to hemoglobin in red blood cells. This oxygen-rich blood is then transported to tissues and organs, providing fuel for cellular metabolism. The diaphragm and intercostal muscles play an important role in this process by contracting and relaxing to ease the flow of air into and out of the lungs.

Slow, deep breaths stimulate the parasympathetic nervous system, encouraging relaxation and helping to alleviate stress. Conversely, rapid, shallow breathing activates the sympathetic nervous system, leading to heightened alertness and stress responses.

The Physics of Breath

The rules of physics help explain the process of breathing when we look into how the mechanics of airflow, pressure gradients, and gas exchange all apply in the process of respiration. When you inhale, the diaphragm contracts and compresses downward, creating negative pressure within the thoracic cavity. This pressure difference causes air to flow into the lungs, filling the alveoli. Exhalation, on the other hand, involves the relaxation of the diaphragm and intercostal muscles, allowing the elastic recoil of the lungs to expel air.

Throughout the respiratory tract, the principles of fluid dynamics apply as air flows from regions of higher pressure to regions of lower pressure. Any resistance encountered along the airways affects the efficiency of breathing. Understanding the physics of breath is critical for improving respiratory function and developing effective breathwork practices.

Quantum Mechanics and Breath

Quantum mechanics is a field of physics that studies the behavior of tiny objects, such as atoms and subatomic particles. It addresses how these particles connect and change energy in ways that conventional physics can't explain. In quantum mechanics, objects can be in multiple places at once, and they can instantly affect each other even when they're far apart. This phenomenon is known as quantum entanglement.

Now, how does this connect to breathing? Every time you breathe, you're taking in air that's made up of tiny particles. These particles have quantum connections to the rest of the cosmos. When you breathe out, you're sending out particles that might become connected to others. This creates an invisible web linking you to everything else in the universe.

Another important part of quantum mechanics is that observing some particles may change them. We can observe this in the double-slit experiment, where atomic particles behave differently when they are being observed compared to when they are not being monitored (Yousif, 2016). Similarly, the act of consciously breathing and being aware of doing so may have a subtle impact on the quantum connections within and around us. When you pay attention to your breath, you might be influencing these quantum particles in some way, even if it's just a little bit. Again, in brief, breathing is more than just receiving oxygen; it allows you to engage with the entire universe on a quantum level.

Having looked into the spiritual and scientific aspects of breathing, the latter from the perspective of biology, physics, and quantum mechanics, we can confidently see how the two combine to create a holistic understanding of the importance of breathing for both our physical and spiritual well-being.

Studies using functional MRI have shown how breath-focused meditation can alter brain activity, increasing connectivity in areas associated with attention and emotional control (Zhang et al., 2023). This increased connectivity may lead to improved cognitive function and emotional regulation. We have also seen how spiritual practices such as pranayama and mindfulness breathing can help reduce stress and anxiety, leading to better mental health and well-being.

Ultimately, integrating both scientific research and spiritual practices surrounding breath highlights the interconnectedness of mind, body, and spirit in achieving optimal health and wellness. This fusion creates an understanding of how all life is connected. Appreciating both science and spirituality opens a richer, more comprehensive experience of the cosmic breath, leading to incredible personal and spiritual growth.

Practical Applications

Breathwork isn't just theory or history; it has real-world uses that can be integrated into everyday life to help you heal and develop self-confidence and awareness. In this section, we will focus on some techniques and exercises you can easily try to help you experience the power of breathwork.

Did you know you can identify unconscious habits and make the necessary health adjustments for your well-being through breath observation? Breathing self-observation is the practice of becoming aware of your breathing patterns and how they relate to your physical, emotional, and mental states.

You can start this practice by setting aside a few minutes each day, sitting quietly, and observing your breath without trying to change it. Notice the depth, rhythm, and quality of your breathing. Is your breathing shallow or deep? Is your breath smooth and even, or is it irregular and strained?

This technique helps you become more aware of your body's signals and how stress, emotions, and daily activities affect your breathing. As you increase your awareness, you will begin to consciously manipulate your breath to promote relaxation and balance within your body. For example, if you notice you're breathing rapidly during stressful situations, you can practice deep, slow breathing to calm your nervous system. There are several breathing exercises for you to practice in the last chapter.

These breathwork practices are structured techniques designed to improve your physical, emotional, and spiritual health. They vary from simple breathing exercises to more advanced techniques found in various healing traditions, which we will look at later.

One easy-to-follow breathwork exercise is the 4–7–8 technique, where you breathe in for four seconds, hold for seven seconds, and then exhale for eight. This method can quickly ease anxiety and encourage relaxation.

Holotropic breathwork is another effective but advanced practice requiring guidance from a certified trainer. This method utilizes fast, deep breathing to reach an altered state of consciousness and access the deeper layers of your psyche. This method is used for personal growth, healing trauma, and spiritual exploration. In a later chapter dedicated to advanced breathwork practices, we will get into more detail on this and other advanced techniques.

As you learn and practice these breath exercises, remember to integrate them into your daily life. You can easily start your day with a few minutes (two to five) of deep, conscious breathing to set a positive tone for your day. As your day progresses, you can set aside breath breaks by simply taking a few deep breaths before a meeting or during a stressful moment.

You can also incorporate breath awareness into physical activities like walking, yoga, or exercise. Focus on coordinating your breath with your movements; this will ensure a smooth and steady flow of oxygen to your muscles and organs. Breathing techniques can help relax your mind and body before promoting deep restful sleep.

The Life Pulse

Consider for a moment how your breath and the energy that flows through your body work in tandem. The life pulse, or energy, flows through your lungs and energizes your body. It is like the battery that interconnects you with the cosmos. Barbara Brennan describes the life pulse as the natural rhythm and energy flow within the body (Brennan, 1990). This pulsation helps connect us on a physical, emotional, and spiritual level.

The life pulse consists of four parts: expansion, stasis and contraction, stasis. When energy expands, it moves away from our core. When it contracts, it moves back inside our core. This rhythm is occurring all the time, even if we don't realize it. When you consciously breathe in, you support the expansion phase; when you consciously breathe out, you promote the contraction phase.

When your breathing aligns with your life pulse, it can help balance your energy, promote natural healing processes, reduce stress and tension, and improve self-awareness. During stressful or traumatic experiences, the life pulse can become disrupted, leading to patterns of contracted breath and energy stagnation. With the right breathwork techniques, you can gently release these contractions and re-establish a healthy flow of energy.

This understanding empowers you to use breath as a tool for healing and transformation. Whether dealing with physical pain, emotional distress, or spiritual challenges, breathwork can provide relief and support in navigating through difficult experiences.

Now that we've covered the fundamentals of breathwork, let's journey across time and space to explore the applications of this knowledge in both ancient times and the present. This combination of old and new views is helpful in gaining knowledge about the potential of breath as we prepare to embrace advanced breathwork techniques.

Chapter 2:

Ancient Wisdom and Modern Insights

The more you know about the past, the better prepared you are for the future. –Theodore Roosevelt

In the previous chapter, we touched on the historical and cultural aspects of breathwork, establishing that this phenomenon is not a new concept and has deep roots in ancient traditions and practices. Before we look into how we currently apply breathwork and its different techniques, developed by modern holistic healers such as Barbara Brennan and Stanislav Grof, we will briefly uncover how ancient civilizations, traditional healing methods, sacred rituals, and mythologies have shaped our understanding of this powerful practice.

We are now aware that breathwork has been an integral part of human culture and spirituality for millennia, and that ancient civilizations recognized the power of breath and developed sophisticated practices to harness its benefits.

Historical Practices

In many ancient civilizations, breath was considered the driving force behind life itself. In ancient Egypt, the concept of ka represented the vital essence or spirit, which was closely linked to breath. The Egyptians practiced deep breathing techniques as part of their spiritual rituals to connect with their gods and achieve higher states of consciousness. An example is solar breath, which involves visualizing the breath as golden sunlight entering the body. This was done because it was believed to infuse the practitioner with divine energy and vitality. Egyptian hieroglyphs and medical papyri suggest that breath was a key concept in their spiritual and healing practices.

Similarly, breathwork was integral to religious and therapeutic practices in the ancient Indigenous civilizations of the Americas. For example, the Lakota people of the Great Plains practiced controlled breathing in ceremonies such as the Inipi (sweat lodge) and "vision quest." This was done as part of purification, spiritual guidance, and the gaining of knowledge.

Additionally, philosophers in ancient Greece associated breath with the spirit of life, particularly during the Hellenistic era. Their belief in the soul and the universe was founded on the concept of "pneuma," or breath. The physical and religious aspects of breathing were the primary focus of philosophers like Galen and Hippocrates, who laid the groundwork for Western medicine and its appreciation of the mind–body connection.

Throughout history, humans have practiced sacred or holy rituals to connect our physical world to the spiritual realms. These rituals often used breathwork to achieve the desired goal. Let us look at some of these ancient rituals.

Eleusinian Mysteries in Ancient Greece

The Eleusinian Mysteries were annual sacred ceremonies held in ancient Greece, particularly in the city of Eleusis. These rites were dedicated to the goddesses Demeter and Persephone and were believed to bring initiates closer to the gods, promising them a better afterlife. The Mysteries involved a series of secretive and elaborate ceremonies, which included fasting, processions, and the ingestion of a kykeon, a special drink believed to induce altered states of consciousness (Tareen, 2022).

Breathwork played a crucial role in these ceremonies. Participants used controlled breathing techniques to enter meditative states, enhancing their spiritual experiences. The rhythmic breathing helped them to focus their minds, release physical tension, and connect more deeply with the divine energies present during the rituals.

Fire Rituals in Hinduism

In Hinduism, breathwork is a big part of fire rituals or yajnas. The purpose of these ceremonies is to offer prayers and offerings to various deities by invoking the power of Agni, the god of fire.

As part of these rituals, participants use synchronized breathing to make their prayers and offerings more powerful. Breath is seen as a vehicle for transporting their intentions and desires to the Divine. Breathing techniques involve deep, rhythmic breathing patterns that help attendees enter a focused and meditative state. This state of heightened awareness allows them to channel their energy and intentions more effectively, ensuring that their prayers are heard and answered. It is also believed that controlled breathing helps to purify the mind and body, making participants more receptive to divine blessings.

Qigong in Chinese Practices

The concept of cosmic breath is deeply intertwined with ancient Chinese practices, including Qigong and Tai Chi. Both disciplines have been practiced for thousands of years, rooted in Taoist philosophy, which emphasizes the balance of energy, or "Qi" (pronounced "chee"), within the body and the universe. Tai Chi, often described as "meditation in motion," incorporates slow, deliberate movements that are synchronized with controlled breathing.

This practice helps cultivate and regulate the flow of Qi throughout the body, promoting physical health, emotional balance, and spiritual harmony. In both Tai Chi and Qigong, the breath is not only a vital life force but also a direct connection to the cosmic energy that permeates all things. By aligning one's breath with the universe, practitioners believe they can achieve a state of balance and unity with the world around them. While these ancient traditions have shaped much of Chinese medicine and philosophy, we will delve deeper into the significance of the cosmic breath and its connection to Qigong in Chapter 4.

Dhikr in Islam Religion

Sufism, a mystical branch of Islam, uses a breathwork practice known as dhikr, or the remembrance of God. To achieve transcendental bliss and oneness with God, practitioners chant the names of God while breathing in a rhythmic pattern. This exercise helps focus the mind, connect the heart and soul, and deepen the connection with the divine presence.

From these sacred rituals, we can see the common goal among the different cultures and beliefs: to achieve spiritual enlightenment and unity with the Divine through the practice of breathwork. This universal pursuit of inner peace and connection to a higher power transcends cultural boundaries and unites humanity in a shared quest for spiritual fulfillment.

Mythologies and Legends

In many creation stories that have been passed down through history, breath has always been portrayed as the divine force that brings life into existence. Earlier, we explored one of the most well-known examples, found in the Judeo–Christian tradition in the book of Genesis 2:7, which states, "And the Lord God formed man of the dust of the ground, and breathed into his nostrils the breath of life, and man became a living soul" (The Holy Bible, New King James Version, 1982).

Similarly, in ancient Egyptian mythology, the god Atum is said to have created the world through his breath. According to Egyptian mythology, the universe was created when Atum, one of the first gods, rose from the primordial abyss and breathed life into the air (Patterson, 2021).

In Greek mythology, the god Prometheus is credited with creating humanity from clay and showering life upon them. According to the legend, Prometheus molded human beings and gave them the breath of life, animating his creations (Atsma, n.d.).

In Māori mythology in New Zealand, the god Tāne Mahuta is said to have breathed life into the first woman, Hineahuone, after forming her from the Earth's clay (Tukiri, 2023). This act of breathing life into clay figures is a recurring theme in many creation myths, symbolizing the divine connection between breath and life.

These myths and legends from diverse cultures highlight the universal belief in the power of breath as a divine force that creates, sustains, and transforms life.

Modern Interpretations

Breathwork has found new life in healthcare and social movements in our modern world. These modern applications expand upon ancient wisdom by integrating breathing techniques into a variety of disciplines that aim to improve our mental, emotional, and spiritual health.

Many rituals and practices have become a lost art whereas others have emerged as essential practices for health and wellbeing. For instance, yoga, which is an ancient practice in pranayama, is used in sessions to improve focus, enhance physical performance, and promote relaxation. Popularized in the early 1960's by the Beatles, Elvis and other celebrities, meditation practices were incorporated to enhance creativity and reduce stress. Today, internationally there are several types of meditation retreats that incorporate breathwork, yoga, and other types of practices to revitalize the body and release emotional and psychological stress. Modern yoga studios offer dedicated breathwork classes alongside physical postures and meditation, acknowledging the importance of breathwork.

Meditation retreats are another popular modern ritual that incorporates breathwork. During these retreats, participants deepen their meditation practice, release emotional blockages, and experience heightened states of consciousness through breathwork exercises. Corporate wellness programs have also begun appreciating breathwork sessions due to their effectiveness in stress reduction and increasing productivity. Some companies offer lunchtime breathwork classes or integrate brief breathing exercises into regular meetings to help employees manage stress and maintain focus. Breathwork has also found its way into the world of professional sports. Many athletes and teams now employ breathing coaches to optimize performance, manage pre-competition nerves, and improve recovery times. This shows the growing recognition of breathwork's potential in high-pressure environments.

New Age Movements

Most New Age movements appreciate and emphasize the importance of ancient breathwork practices, making them accessible to a broader audience. Dedicated to personal development, healing, and happiness, these movements often combine aspects of many spiritual traditions.

Dr. Wilhelm Reich was the first medical doctor to use breathwork in the New Age (Stolkiner, 1997). Reich was a notable psychiatrist and a student of Sigmund Freud; his work focused on the human body and emotions. He came up with the idea of character armor, which implies that emotional inhibition may be reflected in muscular rigidity. In his practice, he systematically used controlled breathing. This led him to observe that many of his patients had insufficient breathing patterns—they would hold their breath or have difficulty exhaling. Reich noted that this caused patients to have stiff and contracted chests, and after being encouraged to breathe out, they started releasing suppressed feelings.

Reich's innovative approach employed specific breathing exercises to release tension and free his patients' emotions, providing psychological healing. His revolutionary work laid the foundation for future practitioners and inspired many who would build upon his methods: notable figures like Alexander Lowen, who developed bioenergetics; Stanislav Grof, who created holotropic breathwork; and Barbara Brennan, who furthered Reich's work with her energy healing techniques.

Stanislav and Christina Grof created holotropic breathwork, one of the ground-breaking New Age breathwork techniques, in the late 1960s (Miller & Nielsen, 2015). Holotropic breathing aims to access the unconscious mind, allowing you to heal trauma and achieve personal transformation. We will get into more detail on this in Chapter 4.

Another well-known breathwork practice in the New Age is rebirthing breathwork, which Leonard Orr introduced. This method focuses on conscious connected breathing to release emotional blockages and traumas, often linked to birth experiences (Watson, 2019). Re-experiencing and processing these early traumas allow you to reach great healing and spiritual awakening.

Brennan Healing Science has also significantly influenced New Age breathwork. Barbara Brennan, a former NASA physicist, developed a comprehensive approach to healing that integrates breathwork with energy healing techniques. Her methods, detailed in her books *Hands of Light* (Brennan, 1990) and Light Emerging (Brennan, 1993), focus on the importance of breath in clearing energy blockages and restoring balance to the body's energy field. Brennan's work has been influential in New Age circles, providing a scientific framework for understanding the energetic dimensions of breathwork.

Other practices, such as transformational breathing and vivation, which combine breath control with affirmations and visualization techniques to improve self-awareness and emotional control, have also been fundamental in the New Age of holistic healing and personal development.

Integrative Medicine

In our modern age, traditional Western medicine appreciates more than ever the value of breathwork in health management across almost all fields of medicine. For example, in obstetrics, midwives and doulas often use breathwork to support expectant mothers during pregnancy and labor. Usually, they advise women to use visual aids, patterned breathing, and deep diaphragmatic breathing to help control pain, lower anxiety, and encourage relaxation. A study revealed that controlled breathing during labor helps facilitate a smoother birthing process by assisting mothers to stay calm and focused, reducing labor time and the need for medical interventions (Heim & Makuch, 2023).

Furthermore, breathwork is now widely practiced in pain management. Deep and slow-paced breathing has been proven to help alleviate chronic pain conditions by reducing muscle tension, improving oxygenation, and triggering the body's relaxation response (Hebert, 2012).

Moreover, breathwork techniques are becoming a key component of cardiac rehabilitation. Techniques such as paced breathing and pursed lip breathing effectively improve lung function and support heart health, benefiting people who are recovering from heart surgeries or heart attacks or managing chronic obstructive pulmonary disease (COPD) (Ramos et al., 2009). Even though breathwork is ancient, the evidence presented above shows its importance in modern healthcare for practitioners and people seeking medical intervention.

Contemporary Spiritual Leaders

In this section, we will focus on contemporary spiritual leaders who have heavily contributed to popularizing and advocating breathwork in our daily lives. Their teachings center on the power of being fully present in the moment and the link between healthy breathing and emotional, mental, and spiritual wellness.

Thich Nhat Hanh, a Vietnamese Zen master and peace activist, is a prominent advocate of mindfulness and breath awareness. In his teachings, he discusses the importance of conscious breathing to anchor oneself in the present moment. He describes how mindful breathing can transform negative emotions and cultivate peace and happiness. His simple yet profound practice of "Breathing in, I calm my body. Breathing out, I smile" has helped countless people integrate breath awareness into their daily lives (Kornbluth, 2023).

Eckhart Tolle, a spiritual teacher and author, also highlights the value of breath in achieving presence and rising above the ego. His teachings center on how conscious breathing can help you disconnect from the constant stream of thoughts and enter a state of heightened awareness and inner peace. He encourages people to use their breath as a way to access the present moment and connect with their true selves.

Pema Chodron was the first fully ordained American female Buddhist nun and teacher. In her practice, Chodron stresses tonglen, a meditation technique that involves breathing in the suffering of oneself and others and breathing out compassion and healing. This practice helps develop empathy, kindness, and emotional and spiritual healing.

These modern spiritual leaders have demonstrated breathwork's positive influence on our state of mind, physical health, and personal development by making it approachable and pertinent to modern audiences.

Applying Ancient Wisdom Today

At this point, we have exhausted ancient breathwork practices and how they fit into the modern world. In this closing section, we will focus on applying this wisdom in daily life and how it can help with personal transformation in daily use.

You are now equipped with reasonable background knowledge of breathwork. Is there any significance to it? How can you be receptive to this life-changing practice? Different spiritual scriptures encourage seeking wisdom and understanding. From the Quran, Surah Al-Baqarah (2:269) states: "He grants wisdom to whom He pleases, and he to whom wisdom is granted receives indeed a benefit overflowing" (The Noble Quran, 1997/n.d.). Similarly, according to the Bible, "Wisdom is the principal thing; therefore, get wisdom, and with all thy getting, get understanding" (The Holy Bible, New King James Version, 1982, Proverbs 4:7).

These scriptures show the value of wisdom and its role in making life easier. Abandoning this wisdom may lead to an unfulfilled life without unlocking your full potential. In Christianity, the Bible quotes, "My people perish for lack of knowledge" (The Holy Bible, New King James Version, 1982, Hosea 4:6). Without the proper understanding and application of knowledge, we may deprive ourselves of a quality life. To open your mind to this life-changing practice, start with small steps. Educate yourself about different breathwork techniques, experiment with them, and observe how they impact your well-being. Be consistent and patient with the practice so you can reap its benefits. Further, consistency will encourage introspection, helping you connect with your inner self and take control of your life.

Incorporating Rituals

Implementing breathwork rituals doesn't require following any religion or culture, or a complete lifestyle overhaul; simple, easy changes can bring the benefits of these ancient rituals into your everyday routines.

One practical approach is to create a daily ritual focused on breathwork. For example, you might start your day with a simple 5–10-minute pranayama practice. Begin with deep belly breathing for a few minutes to center yourself. Then, practice alternate nostril breathing to balance your energy and clear your mind for the day ahead. Another way to incorporate rituals is through transitional breathing. Before starting a new task or entering a meeting, take three conscious breaths. This short ritual draws inspiration from Buddhist mindfulness techniques and can help you approach each new situation with more presence and clarity.

You can also use this ancient wisdom to connect with nature. Take a few minutes each day to step outside and practice conscious breathing. Feel the air entering your lungs, imagining it connecting you to the natural world around you. When you're feeling overwhelmed, practice a simple version of transformational breathing, which we will cover when looking at advanced breathing techniques in Chapter 4. You can do this by taking deep, continuous breaths through your mouth for two to three minutes, allowing any emotions to surface and be released.

Personal Transformation

Personal transformation can be thought of as major changes that occur within us, leading to a new way of being and interacting with the world. You can compare this transformation to that of a butterfly, which undergoes a process called metamorphosis. A butterfly has an interesting evolution cycle from egg to caterpillar to pupa, then into a beautiful and free creature. This process symbolizes growth, change, and discovering your true potential. Even though you won't grow colorful wings like a caterpillar will, breathwork practices can catalyze personal transformation, focusing on deep inner work and emotional release.

You can be open to personal transformation through simple adjustments, such as regular practice or being in a supportive environment. Consistency is key: Set aside time daily for breathwork. This can be just a few minutes, as stated in some of the simple exercises we've looked at. Pick a peaceful, comfortable place where you can practice without interruptions. You will also need to open yourself up to change and go through the process with a willing heart and mind, letting yourself learn and grow. Consider contacting a breathwork coach or signing up with a group for more in-depth understanding and encouragement.

Building on ancient wisdom and modern discoveries, in the next chapter we will turn our attention to how our breathing connects us to the universe in physical and metaphysical ways.

Chapter 3:

Physical and Metaphysical Dimensions

The part can never be well unless the whole is well. –Plato

Understanding the relationship between the physical and metaphysical bodies is critical as you look forward to reaping the full benefits of breathwork. The physical body consists of anatomical structures that help maintain and sustain life in all biological beings. On the other hand, the metaphysical dimension refers to the nonphysical aspect of our existence. This includes energetic, spiritual, and consciousness-based dimensions inside us, such as chakras, energy fields, and auras. These concepts in the metaphysical dimension are important in determining our health and energy levels.

In this chapter, we will concentrate on the relationship between your physical body and the metaphysical dimension. This will help you understand experiences and phenomena that conventional science cannot fully explain, such as intuition, spiritual experiences, and energetic healing.

The Physical Body and Breath

To understand the connection between the physical and metaphysical dimensions, we will begin by breaking down your physical body's anatomy and how it supports breathing. This requires us to look into the respiratory system and the various organs and muscles that make breathing possible. We will break this system down in the simplest way so you can easily understand it. We will focus on the nasal cavity and mouth, the pharynx and larynx, the roles of the lungs, diaphragm, and respiratory muscles, and how these processes supply oxygen to vital organs like the brain and heart. Let's examine the body organs that make breathing possible.

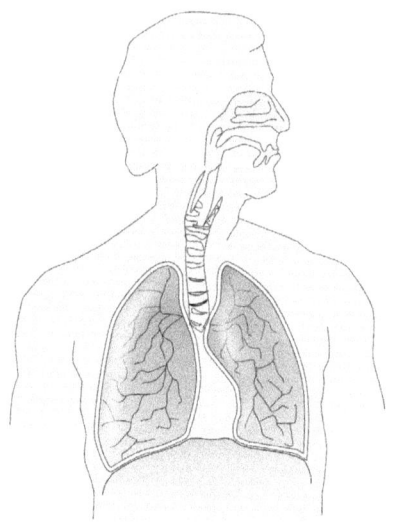

Breathing begins with your nose and mouth, which are the entry points of air into your body. The nasal cavity consists of your nose and sinuses, which help to filter dust and other pollutants. This cavity also helps to warm and humidify the air before it proceeds to your lungs. Additionally, the mouth serves as a different entry point for air, particularly when you are exercising or have a blocked nose from the flu. However, air taken in through the mouth bypasses the above filtration process before it enters the respiratory system.

After entering through the nose or mouth, air travels to the pharynx, a structure in your throat. The pharynx is a muscular tube that serves as a passage for air and food. After this, a small cartilage structure called the epiglottis helps direct the flow of both food and air in your throat. When swallowing, the epiglottis covers the top of the larynx, which is the passage air uses to reach the trachea and then the lungs. This structure prevents food and liquids from entering the airway by directing them into the esophagus, which leads to the stomach. When breathing, the epiglottis remains open to let air flow into the larynx. The larynx houses the vocal cords, which vibrate to create sound when you speak.

The trachea, or windpipe, is a tube that connects the larynx to the bronchi of the lungs. It has hair-like structures and mucus that trap and expel particles and pathogens. The trachea allows the passage of air in and out of your lungs. The trachea divides into two main bronchi, each serving one of the lungs (right and left). These bronchi further subdivide into smaller branches called bronchioles, ensuring air is distributed throughout the lungs. The bronchioles terminate in small air sacs called alveoli.

Your lungs are two spongy, air-filled organs situated in your chest. They contain hundreds of millions of alveoli, which are tiny air sacs. Each alveolus is encircled by a network of small blood vessels called capillaries. When air reaches the alveoli, oxygen passes through their thin walls and into the capillaries. Capillaries carry oxygen-rich blood to the rest of your body while simultaneously picking up carbon dioxide for transportation to the alveoli to be exhaled.

The Respiratory Muscles

The diaphragm is a dome-shaped muscle positioned beneath your lungs, dividing your chest from your abdominal cavity. It is the main muscle used in breathing. As you exhale, the diaphragm relaxes and shifts upward, returning to its curved position. This action reduces the chest cavity's volume and helps expel air from the lungs. This expansion reduces the pressure inside your lungs compared to the air outside them, causing air to flow into your lungs.

When you exhale, the diaphragm relaxes and moves upward into its dome shape, reducing the space in your chest cavity and forcing air out of your lungs. This process happens automatically, thanks to the signals sent from your brain to your diaphragm through the phrenic nerve.

The muscles of respiration also include accessory muscles that help the main breathing muscles, and these are listed below:

- Sternocleidomastoid and scalene muscles: These are located in your neck and help during heavy breathing, intense exercise, or shortness of breath.

- Intercostal muscles: These muscles, situated between your ribs, assist in expanding and contracting the chest cavity. When you inhale, the external intercostal muscles contract, lifting your ribs upward and outward to create more space in your chest cavity. When you exhale, the internal intercostal muscles contract, pulling your ribs downward and inward to help push air out of your lungs.

- Pectoralis minor: This muscle, located on your chest, assists in lifting your upper ribs during deep breaths.

- Serratus anterior: Located on the sides of your chest, these muscles help lift your ribs when breathing deeply. They assist with forceful breathing—for example, when exercising or coughing. When you exhale forcefully, your abdominal muscles contract, pushing your diaphragm upward and helping to expel air from your lungs quickly.

We have established that breathing is important for survival as it helps deliver oxygen to your body. Recall that oxygen is vital for cellular respiration, a process your body undertakes to produce energy for your cell's functions.

The brain is one of the most oxygen-dependent organs. It uses about 20% of the body's oxygen supply to perform its functions (Rink & Khanna, 2011). Too little or too much oxygen in the brain can affect your memory and mood, and also cause other problems.

The heart also requires a constant supply of oxygen to pump blood effectively. Oxygenated blood travels from the lungs to the heart, which then pumps it throughout the body. This process ensures that every organ receives the oxygen it needs to produce energy.

Other vital organs, such as the liver, kidneys, and muscles, also require oxygen to function properly. The liver uses oxygen to detoxify substances and produce important proteins such as albumin. The kidneys rely on oxygen to filter waste from the blood and maintain electrolyte balance, while muscles need oxygen to generate energy for movement. Overall, oxygen plays a crucial role in the proper functioning of all organs in the body.

Understanding the anatomy of breathing helps you appreciate breathing. Even though breathing is automatic, it is a sophisticated process that allows us to experience life to its fullest. Getting acquainted with your respiratory anatomy lays a foundation for practicing breathwork exercises and enriching your metaphysical experience.

The Metaphysical Body: Chakras

We've dissected the anatomy of the physical body; now it's time to break down the metaphysical body. Unlike your physical structures, the metaphysical body is neither tangible nor visible but rather made up of energy and consciousness, which includes your emotions, thoughts, and spiritual presence. Let's get started on comprehending these phenomenal energy centers.

Energy centers, often called chakras, are rotating fields of energy aligned along the spine. The word "chakra," meaning wheel or disk, originates from the ancient Sanskrit language. These chakras symbolize spinning energy hubs within the body. Remember that you cannot see or touch these energy centers, but you can certainly feel their effects on your physical and emotional well-being.

There are seven primary chakras, each with specific functions and associations:

- Root chakra (Muladhara): The root chakra, positioned at the base of the spine, is linked to feelings of safety and grounding. When properly nurtured, this chakra helps you feel safe and stable by connecting you to the Earth.

- Sacral chakra (Svadhisthana): Positioned just below your belly button, the sacral chakra influences creativity, sexuality, and emotional expression. When correctly balanced, this chakra allows you to experience joy, pleasure, and an out-of-this-world experience with your creativity.

- Solar plexus chakra (Manipura): The solar plexus chakra is situated in the upper abdomen, between the belly button and the sternum. This chakra is responsible for your feelings of empowerment, self-esteem, and willpower. Nourishing this chakra allows you to take control of your life and confidently pursue your goals.

- Heart chakra (Anahata): Positioned at the center of the chest, the heart chakra is linked to love, compassion, and emotional equilibrium. Harnessing this chakra allows you to form meaningful bonds with yourself and others.

- Throat chakra (Vishuddha): Situated at the throat, this chakra regulates communication, self-expression, and honesty. When you correctly balance your throat chakra, you will unlock a level of confidence in how you speak your truth clearly and confidently.

- Third-eye chakra (Ajna): The third-eye chakra is located between your eyebrows and is linked to intuition, insight, and wisdom. When you nurture and open it, you will be able to see where your eyes limit you and access deeper levels of understanding.

- Crown chakra (Sahasrara): Found at the top of your head, the crown chakra is associated with spiritual enlightenment. It allows you to connect with divine wisdom and the universal consciousness.

These chakras are essential for balancing our health, wisdom, spiritual life, and relationships with ourselves and others. Blockages or imbalances in these energy centers can manifest as physical diseases or emotional distress.

Human Energy Consciousness Field

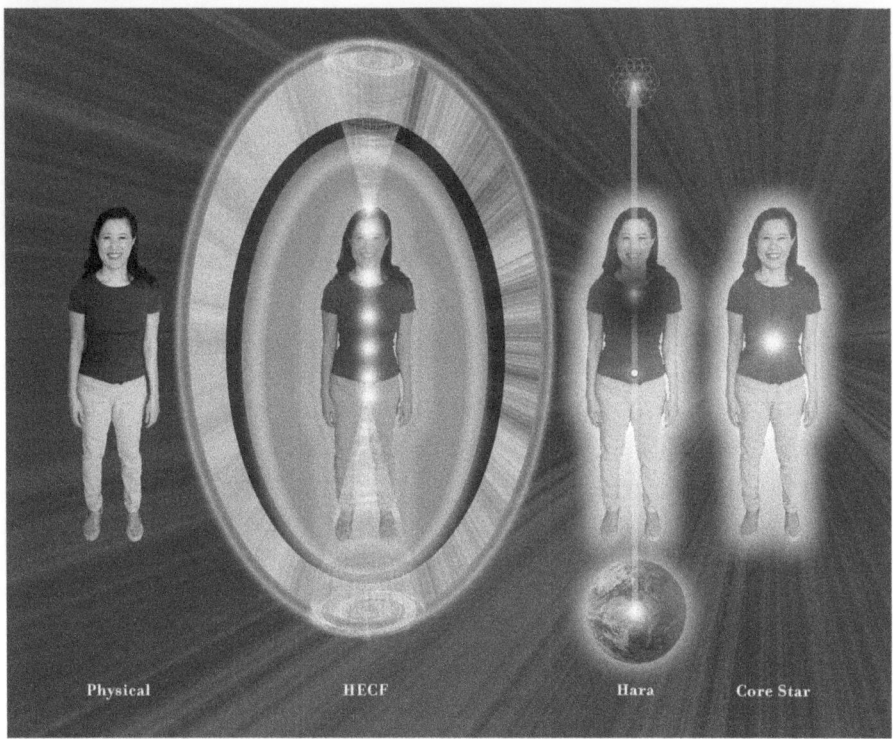

The human energy consciousness field (HECF) is the reflection of the universal energy that is closely connected with your life. It can be described as a light that surrounds and penetrates your physical body. The human energy field radiates a specific type of energy called the aura. Barbara Brennan explains that the aura consists of several layers, each associated with different aspects of the physical, emotional, mental, and spiritual state (Brennan, 1990).

Anatomy of HECF: Let's look at the seven layers of the field and how they interact with your body.

- **Etheric body:** This layer has a form that mimics your physical body. Barbara Brennan describes it as a bluish-gray web of energy lines, a glowing blueprint of your physical body extending about 1/4 to 2 inches from the skin (Brennan, 1990). This layer is associated with physical sensations, including pain and pleasure.

- **Emotional body:** This is the second auric layer. Unlike the etheric body, the emotional body is fluid, doesn't take the form of your physical body, and extends about 1 to 3 inches from the body. It's associated with feelings and emotions. Depending on the energy around you, the colors on this layer range from clear to dark, dull colors. Transparent and highly energized emotions, such as love or excitement, are bright and clear. Feelings of anger or confusion appear dark or dull. Your interpersonal interactions stimulate and have an impact on these feelings.

- **Mental body:** This is the third layer, and it is related to thoughts and mental processes. It extends about 3 to 8 inches from your physical body and is often perceived as yellow light. This layer becomes brighter and more expanded when you're thinking or concentrating.

- **Astral body:** The astral body is the fourth auric layer and is fluid in nature. It extends about 1/2 to 1 foot from your physical body. It is greatly associated with relationships and love and bridges the physical and spiritual worlds. The heart chakra controls the astral layer, which can appear in a range of hues, including red, rose, or orange.

- **Etheric template:** The etheric template is the fifth layer of the human energy field, extending about 1 1/2 to 2 feet from the body. Brennan describes this layer as containing the energetic blueprints or patterns for all physical forms (Brennan, 1990). She likens it to a photographic negative of the body, serving as the blueprint for the etheric layer, which in turn is the template for the physical body. This layer plays a key role in your ability to access the spiritual realm and connect with divine power.

Celestial Body

The sixth layer is semi liquid and spreads approximately 2 to 2 3/4 feet from the body. It is linked with spirituality and high feelings. The celestial body appears as a shimmering light that is mostly gold–silver in color. This is the level through which you may feel spiritual ecstasy.

Ketheric Template

This is the seventh and outer layer, extending approximately 2 1/2 to 3 1/2 feet from your body and appearing as a golden egg shape enveloping all the inner layers. It represents your aura's divine mind, which links to your higher purpose and spiritual essence.

In *Hands of Light*, Brennan emphasizes that these layers are not separate but interpenetrating, each one extending through all the others to your physical body. As you move from the first to the seventh layer, the vibration of the energy becomes finer and higher (Brennan, 1990). She also notes that the perception of these layers often requires different states of consciousness. The lower layers are generally easier to perceive, while the higher layers might require meditative states to observe.

Learning about these layers gives a broad understanding of your physical, emotional, mental, and spiritual state, forming the basis for energy healing practices.

Breathwork Techniques for Cleansing the Aura

You are now oriented to your HECF. Let's briefly look into some techniques for cleaning and protecting your field starting with a cleansing breath. Start by getting into a comfortable position, ensuring that you close your eyes. Specifically, you should imagine that your breath is a light that will cleanse your body of all its toxins. As you breathe in, picture this light penetrating through your body and coming out at the other end. Savor the sensation of cleansing your body, thoughts, and soul. When you breathe out, imagine that all the negative energy, toxins, and anything blocking your aura is coming out with your breath.

Next, we have protective bubble breath. You can practice this in a comfortable sitting or standing position. While focusing on your breath, breathe in and imagine drawing in a warm, golden light that fills your body with protective energy. As you exhale, visualize this golden light expanding outward, forming a protective bubble around your aura. This bubble acts as a shield, safeguarding you from negative energy and maintaining the integrity of your energy field.

Grounding breath is practiced by focusing on slow, deep breaths, this technique helps to ground and stabilize your auric field. As you breathe, imagine roots growing from your feet all the way down into the ground, helping you feel connected and grounded. With each breath, feel these roots anchoring you to the ground, providing stability and a strong connection to the Earth's nurturing energy. This exercise will help you keep your aura centered and balanced.

Then chakra breathing, which improves your energy field, is done by concentrating your breath on the seven chakras, starting with the root chakra and ending with the crown chakra. With each breath, imagine drawing energy into the chakra and lighting it up with bright light. As you exhale, picture this light growing and charging the chakra. This exercise will ensure that the flow of energy within the chakras is harmonized, opening the pathway to healthy living.

Pulsing breath is another exercise. This one exercise requires you to practice deep and slow breathing by inhaling and exhaling in a pattern that is timed and regular. As you slowly breathe, visualize your energy field growing with each breath, then gradually reducing every time you exhale. This pulsing motion helps you energize and fortify your energy field, making it more powerful and alive.

Lastly, color visualization allows you to activate your chakra on the second level of the energy field. While breathing, visualize taking in various colors related to various forms of healing. For example, try to picture yourself breathing in blue to feel less stressed, green to feel centered, or red to feel energized. Imagine these colors permeating your energy field, infusing it with their unique healing properties and helping you balance your emotional and spiritual health.

Energy Healing

Energy healing involves harmonizing the body's energy field to promote healing and balance. You can heal your energy by applying Brennan Healing Science, a comprehensive system that involves using a technique called "rasp breath" to direct, shift, and move energy during a healing session. During this process, you will use your breath to channel and direct energy, making room for healing on multiple levels of your energy field. Let's starting by looking at some specific Breath-Based Techniques in Brennan Healing Science:

Synchronized Breathing

One of the techniques used in Brennan Healing Science is breathing in synchrony. To perform this, an experienced healer will synchronize their breath with yours to create a positive, balanced energy field. The healer is trained to follow your breath and notice the subtle blocks and contractions that may be contributing to your health concerns. The healer guides you into those contracted spaces to release any unresolved or hidden issues. When synchronizing the healer's breath to yours, a morphogenetic resonance occurs where you can release blocked energy and harmonize the field.

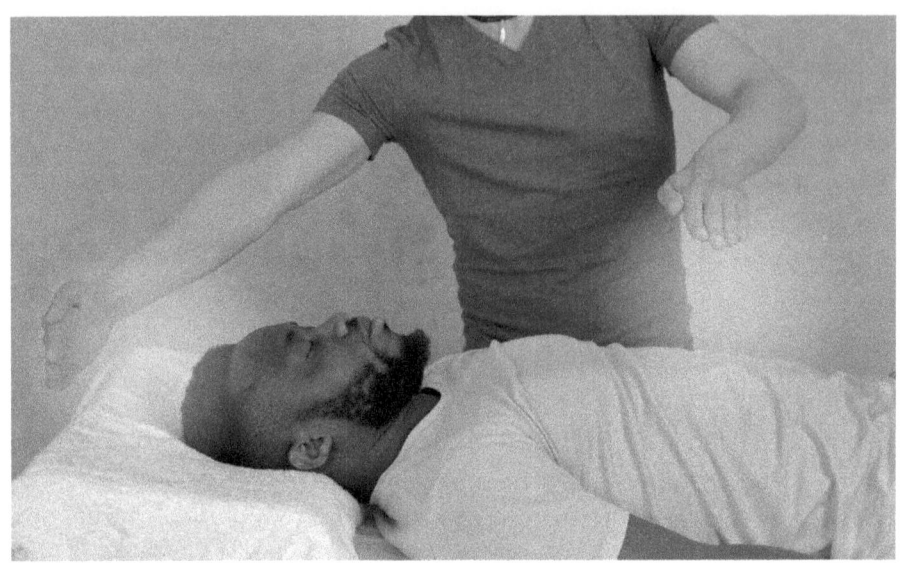

Chelation

This is another breath-based technique where an experienced healer uses color breathing and raspy breath techniques to guide universal energy through your energy field. The healer takes deep, focused breaths; once their field is charged and balanced, they direct this energy through their hands and into your body. This process helps to clear blockages, restore balance, and promote the free flow of your energy. This technique was developed by Rosylyn Bruyere and is described in *Hands of Light*, By Barbara Ann Brennan.

Spiritual Surgery

This is an advanced technique developed by Barbara Ann Brennan that works on your fifth-level aura and involves the healer breathing and charging energy to stay on the fifth level of their energy field, altering their state of consciousness. Through this altered state, the healer can allow higher energy levels to flow into the client's field to repair the fifth-level template. These techniques are used when the client has experienced damage to any of the organs on the physical level, and it leads to extensive healing.

These breathing techniques and healing methods are vital for physical, emotional, mental, and relational health. As well as helping you feel centered and grounded, different types of breathwork assist the healer in establishing the stable and focused state of mind necessary for effective healing work. Additionally, it increases the healer's sensitivity to subtle energies, allowing them to perceive and interact with your energy field more accurately.

With dedicated practice and mindful attention to breathing, anyone can learn to sense and work with the human energy field. This awareness empowers you to take an active role in your healing and personal growth.

Interconnection of Bodies

Now that you are familiar with the physical and metaphysical anatomy, it's time to merge these two aspects to understand their synergistic power. Synergy is when two or multiple components work together to produce an effect greater than the sum of each element. By integrating the physical and metaphysical bodies, you can achieve deeper levels of health and awareness.

The physical and metaphysical bodies are connected in many ways. When you take care of your physical body through proper exercise, diet, and rest, you will improve your physical health and lay a good foundation for nourishing your metaphysical body. Likewise, activities that keep your metaphysical body in shape, such as meditation, energy work, and breathwork, will have a positive impact on your physical body.

For instance, practicing meditation daily helps ease your mind and decrease your blood pressure and stress, which is beneficial for your heart health. Additionally, breathwork can help unclog energetic blocks in your chakra fields; in doing so, you will improve your physical body due to enhanced lung function and oxygenation of tissues. This shows the power of synergizing these two components to achieve a harmonious state that benefits the body and the spirit.

You are now fully aware of how important it is to harmonize your energy on both the physical and metaphysical levels. Let's look at some effective activities that will help you achieve this synchronization:

Grounding Exercises

This type of exercise allows you to connect with the Earth's energy and balance your energy field. This will help you release any excess energy and restore a sense of stability and calmness to your being. To get started, find a quiet place to sit or stand. Close your eyes and take deep, calming breaths. Visualize extending your roots from your feet into the ground. Feel the connection to the ground and the stability it brings. Once you start feeling grounded, visualize any negative energy flowing down through the roots and into the Earth; this will leave you feeling lighter and more centered. Repeat this exercise regularly to maintain a sense of balance and harmony within yourself.

Centering Exercises

These are a powerful way to release negative energy and promote inner peace. You can perform a centering exercise by finding a place where you can sit comfortably with your eyes closed. Place one hand on your heart and the other on your abdomen. Breathe deeply, focusing on the rise and fall of your chest and abdomen. Visualize a bright light from the center of your body growing stronger with each breath. Imagine this light expanding beyond your body, connecting you to the energy of the Earth and the universe. Allow any stress or anxiety to drain into the Earth as you feel yourself firmly planted and supported by the cosmic energy.

Heart Coherence Technique

This is a type of meditation that helps to synchronize your heart rate with your breathing, promoting relaxation and reducing stress. This helps to harmonize your physical and metaphysical body, achieving balance in your energy field. You may begin by sitting quietly and placing your hands over your heart. Breathe slowly and deeply, focusing on the area around your heart. Think of something that brings you joy or gratitude. Continue this focused breathing for several minutes. Imagine a bright, warm glow encircling your heart and spreading outward as you maintain your deep breathing. As you connect to the energy of the universe, a sense of peace and serenity will surround you.

These synergistic activities will help you achieve a balanced and harmonious state that supports your overall well-being.

Balance and Alignment

Other activities that can bring balance and alignment to your physical and metaphysical body include Tai Chi and Qigong. These exercises combine physical movement with breath control and meditation, helping to unify your body and mind. When your body moves in tandem with your breath, you create a flow of energy that connects your physical structure to your energetic field.

For example, maintaining proper posture during meditation supports physical health simply by reducing tension, promoting circulation, and enhancing the flow of energy through your chakras. This balance allows you to access deeper states of meditation and mindfulness, forging a path for emotional and spiritual stability.

Moreover, achieving balance and alignment includes being mindful of your thoughts and emotions. Negative thoughts and feelings can create energetic imbalances that manifest as physical ailments. On the other hand, positive thinking, gratitude, and emotional regulation help you maintain a balanced energy field that supports your overall health.

Freeing the Flow With Cosmic Breath

Let's now focus on the therapeutic power of cosmic breath and its role in maintaining the free flow of energy throughout your body. As we proceed, keep in mind that when the energy field is blocked, the physical body cannot function properly and disease may result. The free flow of energy is vital for your health and well-being—this cannot be emphasized enough. Learning to harness the power of cosmic breath can help to release any blockages in the energy field, allowing for a more balanced and harmonious state of being.

Developing a conscious habit to check in and focus on how you are breathing throughout the day offers you several opportunities to change bad breathing habits. Many of us experienced different types of trauma in early childhood from perhaps a premature birth, loss of a parent, or a traumatic event. These early experiences map into our deep limbic system and respiratory system. These are just beneath consciousness yet impact how we breath. We can unconsciously hold our breath in the upper chest area, diaphragm area or lower abdomen. These patterns stop the life force or life pulse from sending energy to vital parts of our body. Becoming aware that the cosmos and the life pulse of our planet is actually intricately involved in breathing us into life, offers many opportunities to revitalize your health and wellbeing.

Here are a few daily practices you can easily incorporate into your busy schedule. Whether you are at work, riding a bus, flying, or relaxing comfortably at home, these simple breathing exercises can enhance your energy and revitalize your health. You can practice these exercises to promote free flow and maintain the opening and circulation of energy between the physical and metaphysical bodies.

Full Yogic Breath

Also known as three-part breath, this involves inhaling deeply into your abdomen, then expanding your rib cage and, finally, filling your chest with air. This helps to oxygenate your body fully and release any tension or blockages in the energy channels.

To begin, find a comfortable place to sit or lie down. Before making any changes, start by watching your breath's natural rhythms. This practice helps you become aware of any disruptions and refocus on your breathing. Begin by inhaling deeply through your nose, allowing the air to fill your abdomen first, then your chest, and finally your upper lungs. Pause for a moment while holding your breath, then exhale slowly and fully through your nose. Visualize your breath as a wave of energy flowing through your entire body. Feel the tension melting away with each breath, allowing your body to relax more deeply with each exhale. As you continue this deep breathing exercise, imagine any energy blockages being released and replaced with a sense of calm and peace. You can practice this exercise every morning and evening for five to ten minutes.

Circular Breathing

Circular breathing is a powerful technique designed to maintain an uninterrupted flow of air, resulting in a steady circulation of energy throughout the body. Unlike conventional breathing, where there's often a brief pause between inhaling and exhaling, circular breathing eliminates this interruption, creating a seamless and rhythmic cycle of breath.

To practice, begin by inhaling deeply through your nostrils. As you exhale, let the air flow out through your mouth in a continuous, smooth motion without pausing. The goal is to establish an effortless rhythm where your inhales and exhales transition seamlessly. When inhaling, focus on expanding your lungs fully, allowing your chest and diaphragm to open completely. During exhalation, ensure you release the air fully and evenly, maintaining a steady pace.

This technique is particularly beneficial during activities such as yoga, walking, or any repetitive movement where endurance and energy flow are essential. It enhances oxygen delivery, promotes a sense of calm, and helps sustain energy levels, making it an excellent practice for both physical and mental resilience. Circular breathing not only supports your physical performance but also cultivates a meditative state, grounding your mind while invigorating your body. With regular practice, this method can significantly improve your capacity for mindfulness and endurance.

Health Benefits of a Free Breath Flow

Learning how to breathe freely offers numerous benefits that enhance various aspects of your life. It increases energy levels by boosting cellular function through greater oxygen intake, which leads to heightened alertness and activity throughout your day. This practice also helps reduce fatigue, leaving you feeling more energized. Mental clarity is another significant advantage, as free breath flow improves focus and concentration. This leads to better decision-making, enhanced memory, and more efficient information processing.

Additionally, it fosters emotional balance by regulating the autonomic nervous system, reducing anxiety, and promoting emotional stability. As a result, your mood improves, and you become more resilient to emotional stressors. Physically, free breath flow supports the immune system and aids in the body's natural detoxification processes, contributing to overall health. On a spiritual level, it encourages deeper meditative states, enhancing intuition and fostering greater inner awareness.

Mastering the art of breathing can help you overcome obstacles in your life and live up to your full potential by releasing pent-up emotions and revitalizing your body.

One powerful example of this transformation is a 75-year-old woman who sought my help. During one of our meetings, I noticed she had very shallow breathing: Her upper chest barely moved, and no energy moved beyond her diaphragm into her lower abdomen. I asked her if I could place my hand on her belly during this session, and she agreed. I further asked her if she could open her breathing to lift the hand that was placed on her abdomen. It took several attempts for her to breathe through the held contractions in her body. Once she opened her breath fully, she exclaimed with a smile, "Oh my, oh my! I haven't felt those feelings in a long time—since my husband died."

At that moment, she reconnected with her sensuality and sexuality. She realized that she had unconsciously blocked these feelings, believing that her age and the loss of her husband meant she no longer needed to feel such emotions. This realization was an awakening for her, as she understood that her life force and breath could unlock pleasurable feelings and reawaken her body. Over time, societal and personal beliefs had restricted her life force from flowing freely into essential areas of her body.

In my practice, I have worked with many clients who have experienced similar blockages in their life force energy. However, through various advanced breathwork techniques that bring healing energy, I have witnessed transformations in individuals as they release their restrictions and allow their life force to flow freely once again.

I'm sharing this so you can see how integrating physical and metaphysical practices prepares you to understand the cosmic breath's role in personal transformation and bringing about self-empowerment. In the next chapter, you will be empowered with practical knowledge of advanced breathing techniques that will boost your free energy flow and unlock another level of consciousness within yourself.

Chapter 4:

Breathing Techniques and Concepts

Breath is the power behind all things. I breathe in and know that good things will happen. –Tao Porchon-Lynch

The previous chapters have helped us appreciate that breath is a bridge between the body and mind and has much therapeutic potential. In this chapter, we are going to focus on advanced breathing techniques. We will unveil a body-centered approach to breathing, how these methods were developed in recent history, and their therapeutic benefits.

Before we get started, it is worth recalling that Wilhelm Reich was the first to systematically analyze the therapeutic uses of breath in the early 20th century (Stolkiner, 1997). During the same period, he developed a therapy called character analysis vegetotherapy, which uses deep, circular breathing to uncover and process emotions. Character analysis will be explored more in Chapter 6. Reich's approach was innovative, as he believed that freeing the breath could unlock repressed memories and feelings, thus facilitating emotional and psychological healing.

Reich's approach involved working with patients lying on a mat or cushion. However, Alexander Lowen, John Pierrakos, and later Barbara Brennan recognized the importance of having patients stand upright. This position made it easier to identify areas of body armoring and allowed Lowen, Pierrakos, and Brennan to develop body-centered exercises to activate contracted energy, free the life pulse, and open the body's natural energy channels. They designed specific core movement exercises tailored to release different types of body armor and blockages. We will explore these methods in greater detail later in this chapter.

Adding to this newfound movement, Stanislav Grof introduced the idea of holotropic breathwork in the 1970s (Fortier, 2022), which we will explore shortly. In keeping with the view that breathwork can significantly affect one's physical and spiritual well-being, this method further emphasizes the powerful relationship between breathing, awareness, and treatment.

All the work mentioned above had a tremendous impact on Barbara Brennan, who applied these principles in her energy healing framework and techniques. Her method emphasizes that true health is more than just the physical body; it also includes the human energy consciousness system, which integrates the mind, body, and soul. These pioneers established the framework for modern advanced breathing practices, each building on their predecessors' findings to deepen our awareness of the vital function of breath in healing and transformation.

During the initial stages of breathwork, you might hyperventilate as your body adjusts to the new breathing patterns. As you become more familiar with breathwork, your body's response will begin to normalize, and the sensations of hyperventilation and associated symptoms will decrease. With regular practice, your body will develop a more natural and balanced breathing rhythm. With experience, breathwork will become a seamless part of your routine and it will become easier to regulate your breathing during stressful situations.

Can you tell the difference between prolonged, contracted breath and a medical emergency? Although we have discussed some signs of medical emergencies that may occur during a session, it's also important that you don't confuse prolonged contracted breath with an emergency. Unlike the distress symptoms seen in hyperventilation, there may be chest tightness and difficulty taking deep breaths when you are in a prolonged contracted state, but typically there is no dizziness or lightheadedness. It is important to stay calm and focus on slowing down your breathing in these situations.

Precautions for Breathwork Practice

Even though breathwork is safe for most people, if you have certain conditions, I recommend you consult with a medical professional before starting any breathwork practice. Some of the conditions you need to be aware of are Cardiovascular conditions, Respiratory conditions, Pregnancy, and Seizure disorders. As with any other powerful tool, breathwork should be used with respect and care. If you attempt these exercises incorrectly, you may have a negative experience with them. Before we discuss these techniques in detail, it is important to consider the possible risks of breathwork, how to spot them, and what to do if you encounter them. If breathwork is not done correctly, it can cause hyperventilation, paresthesia, tetany, and syncope. Let's examine these side effects closely.

First, we will look at hyperventilation. It is mostly characterized by rapid breathing that can lead to dizziness and fainting. This may occur as you are getting acquainted with breathing techniques. You may experience this due to blood carbon dioxide levels dropping drastically, which may occur when you breathe too fast or excessively. This drop in carbon dioxide can cause an imbalance in the blood between oxygen and carbon dioxide, raising the blood's pH. This may lead to the manifestation of symptoms such as those listed below:

- dizziness or lightheadedness

- difficulty breathing

- chest pain

- confusion

- feeling suffocated

- visual disturbances

- dry mouth

When you notice that you are hyperventilating, it is important to try to slow down your breathing and focus on taking deep, slow breaths. Another helpful technique involves breathing into a paper bag. To use this method, cover your mouth and nose with the bag and take slow, deep breaths. This helps you re-inhale the carbon dioxide you've just exhaled, restoring balance and alleviating the symptoms. If symptoms still persist after this, seek immediate medical attention.

There is also a risk of paresthesia, which refers to a tingling or numb sensation in the extremities (hands or feet). You may feel like your body is being poked with pins or needles. Hyperventilation may cause paresthesia. While it may be alarming, understanding that it is a temporary effect of lower carbon dioxide levels can help you cope calmly. Paresthesia is usually harmless and goes away once your breathing returns to normal.

Lastly, there is tetany, and it can be seen as involuntary muscle contractions after a prolonged period of hyperventilation, and its symptoms include the following:

- muscle cramps or spasms, particularly in the hands and feet

- stiffness or rigidity in the muscles

- painful contractions

- difficulty controlling movements

If you experience tetany while practicing breathwork, immediately reduce your breathing rate. Start focusing on deep, slow breaths and grounding techniques, which we looked into previously. If necessary, stop the session and allow your body to return to a normal breathing rhythm.

In addition, hyperventilation can lead to other complications if not addressed in a timely manner, including syncope (fainting or loss of consciousness) and stress and anxiety. Hyperventilation-induced vasoconstriction is to blame for this, as it lowers blood flow to the brain and may cause fainting or loss of consciousness. Hyperventilation can also exacerbate stress and anxiety symptoms. It is essential to learn relaxation techniques and get medical assistance if necessary to control these symptoms.

The Main Types of Breathwork

With all the precautionary measures discussed, let's now focus on getting oriented with the types of breathwork practices. As we proceed, you should know that each type of breathwork practice offers benefits that can help you achieve deeper physical, emotional, and spiritual healing. We are going to briefly break down the history, principles, and practical applications of these exercises.

Reichian breathwork is based on Wilhelm Reich's work and focuses on the relationship between a person's body and their emotional state. Its core principles include the release of armor, the connection between breathing and emotion, and the body–mind connection.

Reich believed that emotional blockages caused by unresolved conflicts, trauma, or emotional instability that we try to suppress manifest as physical tension or armoring in the body. This belief led to the development of his breathwork approach, which aims to release armor and allow the free flow of energy and emotions. This practice recognizes the close relationship between your emotional states and breathing patterns. For instance, when you suppress your emotions, your breathing becomes restricted and shallow, but when you release those emotions, your breathing becomes free and full. Therefore, altering your breathing patterns can facilitate the release of deeply suppressed emotions. This eventually leads to self-awareness and reduced physical tension and stress.

Reichian breathwork focuses on belly and chest breathing techniques. Let's look into these in the next section.

Belly Breathing

The belly breathing technique involves breathing deeply into the abdomen, expanding it fully as you inhale. This helps activate your diaphragm, promoting relaxation and emotional release.

To get started, find a quiet, comfortable place and time where you will be uninterrupted. Then, lie on a mat with your knees bent and your feet placed flat on the floor. This will help relax your body and allow full air entry for these exercises. While you're lying down, position one hand on your abdomen and the other on your chest. Breathe deeply through your nose, lifting your abdomen while keeping your chest motionless. Next, exhale slowly through your mouth while feeling your abdomen fall with your hand as you release the air.

Maintain this deep breathing rhythm for five to ten minutes, focusing solely on the movement of your abdomen as it rises and falls with each breath. Keep your rhythm constant and pay attention to any regions in your belly where you feel tense or uncomfortable. This tenseness may be an indication of armoring. Concentrate on letting go of this tightness by allowing your abdomen to expand completely with each inhalation. After the session, you'll feel the tension and stress melt away.

Chest Breathing

Chest breathing focuses on expanding your chest and rib cage with each breath. This helps to release tension in your upper body, which includes your chest, shoulders, and neck, paving the way for better emotional expression.

To do this, lay on your back—as with the belly breathing method—with your feet planted into the ground and your knees up at a 30-40 degree angle. Maintain the same position, with the chest being the center of attention. Inhale deeply through your nose, focusing on expanding your chest while keeping your abdomen relatively still. Next, slowly release the air through your mouth as you feel your chest flatten with your hands.

Keep focusing on breathing into your chest for the next five to ten minutes. Maintain a steady rhythm and notice any areas in your chest that feel tight or restricted. This might indicate armoring in your upper body, just like in the abdomen. Work on releasing this tension by allowing your chest to expand fully with each inhalation. As you focus, you will feel a sense of openness and release in your chest, shoulder, and neck area as tension leaves your body.

Belly and Chest Combination

When participating in breathwork exercises, breathing through your nose rather than your mouth is a better choice for your well-being. Nose breathing filters and warms the air, supporting lung health and aiding in calming your mind by activating the parasympathetic nervous system. In contrast, mouth breathing bypasses these benefits, leading to potential respiratory infections and disruption of your energy flow. Choosing nose breathing will help you harness your breath's full power, enhancing your physical and spiritual health.

As you continue your practice, you can also combine the two exercises above into one practice. Get started by maintaining a lying-down position. Switch between belly and chest breathing every few breaths, following the steps above for each one. This combination will help you achieve relaxation and release more tension from your body. Think of it as the synergy of two workouts.

As you keep practicing this exercise, you will become able to maintain a sense of self-awareness and mindfulness in your regular breathing patterns, allowing you better to manage stress and anxiety in your daily life. This will eventually lead to a better quality of life.

The duration of belly and chest combination breathwork varies depending on your current level:

- For novices, the total practice time is five to ten minutes. Every one to two minutes, you should switch between belly and chest breathing.

- The total duration for those at intermediate level is 15–20 minutes, with three to five minutes dedicated to each type of breathing before switching.

- For those at an advanced level, a session can typically last from 30 minutes to an hour and may involve longer periods of each breathing type.

Although you can do these exercises on your own, it's best to have a trained practitioner lead you in a group or individually. Practitioners can also help identify any of the side effects or complications we looked at earlier, in case you encounter one of them. This will allow for timely intervention.

Brennan Core Process: Breathwork

In the early 1980s, Barbara Brennan, a protege of John Pirrakoss and Alexandar Lowen emerged on the scene as a pioneer in human energy consciousness studies. Her groundbreaking books, *Hands of Light* and *Light Emerging* are foundational in the study of human energy healing work. Her "Brennan Core Process" approach evolved from Reichian therapy and incorporated what she coined as the Four Dimensions of Humankind which later evolved into the Human Energy Consciousness System (HECS).

Over four decades, Brennan evolved her work with trauma and the human energy consciousness system to integrate all the dimensions in the healing process. This work involves understanding how trauma is stored in the body, human biofield, Hara dimension etc. Over four years, students learn the complex chakra system and human energy field while tracking the contracted breath appearing in the body amour. She synthesised her predecessor's work into an approach that identified the developmental reactive personality patterns that appear in the human energy field as the core essence curls in on itself.

Her theory proposes that human dimensions emerged from the core essence of an individual. The hara and human energy consciousness field (HECF), and physical body emerge from the core interpenetrating into the earth dimension. Prior to birth and taking your first breath we are cosmically connected to universal oneness. Our first breath of life is our individuation from the black velvet void of the cosmos, to our mother's womb and into life. Breath is the foundation of life. Any trauma during these stages can cause a restriction or suppressed breathing pattern that may go unnoticed.

Trauma appears on each dimension within the memory field. In *Core Light Healing*, Brennan reframes the concept of trauma as the core light curled in on itself in a creative defensive way. From my perspective it is the core essence of an individual trying to navigate being human. The defensive solution is a response or a reaction to not being met from the dimension of the core essence of the parents, caregivers, teachers etc. This is a highly sophisticated and creative solution that inevitably creates blocks that appear in the Hara Dimension as well as Human Energy Consciousness Field and eventually as dis-ease in the physical body.

In the Brennan Core Process, the practitioner is an energy specialist who is trained to track the creative life pulse through all phases of expansion, stasis and contraction, stasis. Being in sync with the life pulse the practitioner can shift the frequency of energy being transmitted and help release trauma and restore the divine nature of the human energy consciousness system.

Holotropic and Rebirth Breathwork

Holotropic breathing is a practice that involves rapid, deep breathing and evocative music to induce altered states of consciousness, or what is now termed non-ordinary states of consciousness. Stanislav and Christina Grof, a married couple who practiced psychology, created this method in the 1970s. Grof's earlier work, in which he experimented with the therapeutic effects of lysergic acid diethylamide (LSD) on his patients, served as inspiration for this practice (Holmes et al., 1996). After the U.S. government banned the use of LSD, Grof sought to find a safer alternative to achieve similar results, leading to the development of holotropic breathing.

The purpose of this exercise is to find enlightenment from within, helping you achieve a sense of self-awareness, growth, and connection to a higher power. You may experience this feeling of enlightenment in the form of catharsis. Around the world, people have used this practice in a variety of contexts, including therapeutic, spiritual, and personal growth workshops.

What to Expect During Holotropic Breathwork

Before starting, you should ensure a qualified practitioner guides you through this process for a safe and beneficial experience. Most people perform this exercise in groups, but you can also do it individually. While you prepare, your trained facilitator will place you in a comfortable, safe space, where they will introduce you to the process. This preparation helps you understand what to expect and sets your expectations for the session.

A partner or trained facilitator will accompany you, ensuring your safety throughout the process. We refer to the observer as a sitter and you as the breather. If paired with someone else, you can switch these roles. Your facilitator will be guiding you throughout this process, instructing you to engage in deep, rapid breathing to achieve a non-ordinary state of consciousness. Throughout the session, evocative music will be playing; this will help guide you through different emotional and psychological experiences.

A typical holotropic session lasts two to three hours, though some may extend to a full-day workshop. After breathing, you can share your experiences with the group. During your session, you may experience different levels of awareness. You might relive birth experiences and associated traumas, feel physical sensations and movements related to stored memories, and access and process personal life memories and traumas. Your experience will be unique and self-directed. Engaging in holotropic breathwork can lead to you accessing deeper layers of your psyche, emotional release and healing, enhanced self-awareness and spiritual growth, and the integration of past traumas.

Even though this practice is beneficial, some critics argue it can be psychologically destabilizing, especially if you have a history of trauma or mental health problems (Miller & Nielsen, 2015). The intense emotional and physical experiences may not suit everyone. This risk shows the importance of having a qualified guide who can spot this.

Rebirthing Breathwork

Rebirthing is a breathwork practice that involves conscious connected breathing to release emotional blockages and trauma stored in your body. This exercise aids in healing and growth by activating a deep state of relaxation and self-awareness.

Rebirthing breathwork was developed in the 1960s by Leonard Orr as a result of his hypothesis that many of our current life problems are a result of unresolved subconscious traumas that date back to our birth (Phillips, 2009). This exercise focuses on a connected breathing pattern or conscious breathing energy in which there is no pause between the inhale and exhale, creating a continuous loop of breath. As a result, this loop helps oxygenate the brain, activate the parasympathetic nervous system, and stimulate the vagus nerve, leading to a deep state of calm and altered consciousness.

As you prepare to start, you will need a qualified instructor to introduce you to rebirthing breathwork principles. They may also help you set personal intentions for the session. There are various formats for rebirthing sessions based on your age and desired outcomes.

To get started, you will lie down in a comfortable place. Next, you will actively take a deep breath in through your mouth and passively exhale, again through your mouth. You will repeat this sequence without pausing. Mouth breathing is commonly used during this exercise, but this also depends on your practitioner, as some might use a combination of mouth and nose breathing.

As the session continues, you will feel the release of tension from your body and mind. Your instructor will encourage you to observe any physical or emotional sensations without judgment. As you continue, you may experience the surfacing and release of long-held emotions and traumas. This process can be intense, but it is important for healing. Your certified facilitator will be there with you to ensure you remain safe and supported.

This session may last between one and two hours. After the session, you will be encouraged to rest and reflect on your experience; this allows you to absorb the healing effects and integrate any meaningful lessons learned.

Hot Tub Rebirthing

Another form of rebirthing involves immersing yourself in warm water, ideally in a bathtub or hot tub. This practice is also done under the strict supervision of a certified rebirthing instructor. You will lie in the water with your face above the surface during this process. The warm water helps relax your body and evokes a prenatal experience. Your instructor will help you with conscious, connected breathing while in the water. This exercise usually lasts one to two hours. This practice aims to simulate the womb environment and birth experience.

Under correct supervision, rebirthing breathwork is life-transforming. It might help you find buried memories and events in your subconscious, which may help you understand why you feel or act in certain ways. It can also heal you on a mental, physical, and spiritual level. Improperly done, rebirthing breathwork can lead to hyperventilation, dizziness, and even panic attacks. Remember, this exercise should only be done carefully and with the help of a professional to avoid complications and to ensure you have guidance when dealing with repressed pain that may be difficult to process.

Cosmic Breath in Qigong

In traditional Chinese medicine, the health of the body is maintained by ensuring that Qi—the human energy consciousness we mentioned earlier—flows freely throughout the body's meridians. When Qi is blocked or becomes stagnant, illness arises. Cosmic breath helps clear these blockages, promoting healing and vitality. Through Qigong, the practitioner consciously works with their breath to guide Qi through the body, dissolving blockages and improving the flow of energy to all organs and systems.

The effects of regular cosmic breathwork are profound, offering benefits not only for physical health but also for emotional and spiritual growth. Practitioners of Qigong believe that by practicing deep, mindful breathwork, they can tap into the universal Qi, balance their internal energy, and cultivate longevity, peace, and clarity.

The practice of cosmic breath in Qigong has been an integral part of Chinese philosophy and healing for thousands of years. Ancient Chinese wisdom understands the breath as a powerful tool for connecting with the universe and maintaining health. By intentionally harnessing the energy of the cosmos through mindful breath, Qigong practitioners can achieve harmony within themselves and with the world around them. Cosmic breath remains a cornerstone of Qigong and continues to inspire people today to explore the vast potential of breath as a means of healing and self-awareness. (Egberts, 2023).

The origins of QiGong date back over 5,000 years in China, where it evolved from the philosophical and spiritual traditions of Taoism, Confucianism, and Chinese Buddhism. Central to these teachings was the belief that life force or energy, known as "Qi", flows through all living things. Qi is thought to be the vital force that sustains life, and when it flows freely and harmoniously, health and well-being are maintained. However, when the flow of Qi is blocked or disrupted, illness and emotional imbalances occur.

In the ancient Chinese worldview, the universe is alive with energy, and everything is interconnected. Cosmic breath, or "Tian Qi," refers to the breath that connects an individual to the vast energy of the universe. Through Qigong practices, it was believed that the breath could harness and circulate this energy within the body, promoting health, healing, and spiritual awakening.

In Qigong, breath is used intentionally to influence the movement of Qi through the body. The breath is considered a bridge between the physical and the spiritual realms, enabling practitioners to tap into the cosmic energy that permeates the universe. In this practice, breathing is not shallow or automatic; instead, it is deep, slow, and mindful, encouraging the practitioner to move in sync with the natural rhythms of life.

Ancient Qigong masters understood that the quality of the breath affected both the body and mind. They developed specific breathwork techniques designed to calm the mind, release tension, and guide the body into a state of balance. These techniques include:

1. Abdominal Breathing (Diaphragmatic Breathing): This technique involves breathing deeply into the abdomen rather than the chest, allowing the practitioner to fully oxygenate the body and increase the flow of Qi. This method is thought to calm the nervous system and promote inner peace.

2. Reverse Breathing: This advanced technique involves pulling the abdomen in while inhaling and expanding it while exhaling. It's used to strengthen the body's energy field and support internal organs.

3. The "Cosmic Breath" or "Heavenly Breath": This is a specific type of breath in which the practitioner imagines themselves drawing energy from the cosmos with each inhale, and then

releasing stagnant energy from the body with each exhale. The breath aligns with the movement of Qi, guiding it through pathways in the body known as meridians.

The practice of Qigong is deeply connected to Taoism, which emphasizes living in harmony with the Tao (the Way), the underlying natural order of the universe. Taoist philosophy teaches that human beings are microcosms of the larger universe, meaning that the energy that flows through the cosmos is the same energy that flows within our bodies (Hu Fuchen, 2013).

The Taoists believed that breathing, as a means of interacting with Qi, was a sacred practice. They viewed cosmic breath as a way of aligning oneself with the forces of nature, harmonizing the body's energy with the energies of the world around it. Breathing deeply and mindfully connects the practitioner with the Tao, enabling them to align their internal energy with the universal flow. The ancient Taoists were among the first to document and codify breathwork exercises in their texts, such as the *Dao De Jing* and various Taoist medical manuals (Laozi & Chu, 1982).

Transformational Breathwork

Judith Kravitz, a student of Leonard Orr, created this practice in the 1970s as a way to encourage healing and personal development through conscious breathing (Walters, 2023). It focuses on deep, connected breathing patterns to release emotional blockages and improve well-being. It combines conscious breathing, movement, and sound to release emotional obstacles and aids in integrating your body, mind, and spirit. The principle behind it is similar to Reich's theory of emotional release through breathwork, which also helps facilitate emotional and physical healing.

You will have a certified facilitator who will guide you through the process, using techniques such as movement, sound, and acupressure as tools to help release blockages. Their guidance will ensure that you remain safe and supported throughout the process. As you start the session, you will lie down comfortably with your eyes closed and be required to set personal intentions.

Your instructor will then ask you to take deep breaths through your mouth, filling your lungs. As you inhale, you will allow your belly to expand fully. You will then release the breath through your mouth without pausing, letting it flow naturally. You will maintain this circular breathing pattern, inhaling and exhaling through your mouth without any pauses between breaths.

As you breathe, you should keep your throat open and your jaw relaxed. As you exhale, your facilitator will gently guide you to release any tension you feel in your body. As you progress, you will be gently asked to gradually increase the pace of your breathing while ensuring it remains comfortable for you.

Transformational breathwork sessions typically last between one and two hours and can be done individually or in small groups. Always remember to work with a certified instructor to ensure a safe and effective experience. During the session, you might experience an overflow of emotions. If this happens, allow yourself to feel and express them as part of the healing process.

Be aware of any discomfort or unusual physical sensations as you participate in this exercise. If you notice anything, promptly communicate with your facilitator for help. After the session, take time to rest and hydrate. And, if possible, journal or discuss your experience with a trusted friend or facilitator.

This exercise will allow you to release energy blockages, heal emotional wounds, and awaken to your full potential.

Vivation

This is a practice developed by Jim Leonard and Phil Laut (1991). This method combines conscious breathing and feeling awareness to help you overcome negative emotions and improve your overall well-being.

The core principle of this exercise is to help you process and integrate your emotions through a structured breathing practice. This practice discourages the suppression of emotions; instead, it encourages the transformation of emotional challenges into opportunities for growth and positive energy. Unlike other breathwork practices that might focus solely on catharsis, vivation encourages a gentle, mindful approach to working with emotions.

Your certified instructor will first introduce you to the principles of vivation and assist you in setting personal outcome goals for the session. Your facilitator will then help you get comfortable by asking you to lie down or recline. You will begin the session by breathing slowly and deeply through your nose, allowing your abdomen to rise and fall. It would help if you focused on the sensation of the breath moving in and out.

As the session continues, you will be encouraged to use conscious, connected breathing—breathing in and out deeply and more audibly, continuously, without a break. This ongoing flow of breath helps release and transform stored emotions.

As you exercise, you will need to focus on any emotions you feel and avoid suppressing them. This will enable you to experience and accept them fully. Then, you will take that negative feeling and start turning it into positive energy. This will result in you feeling a balance of emotions and joy.

These sessions have a duration of one to two hours. You have the option to have a one-on-one session with your facilitator or to practice with a small group of other people. Your instructor will be present to help you manage your emotions safely and effectively throughout the process.

The exercise will end with your instructor helping you reflect on your progress and adopt a positive outlook. This will help you continue to cultivate emotional balance and joy in your daily life.

As we conclude this chapter, remember that the way we breathe holds incredible power over our physical, emotional, and mental well-being. The practical exercises you've explored here are more than just techniques—they're tools for transformation. Whether you're seeking to find calm in the chaos, boost your energy, or reconnect with yourself, these breathing practices can make a profound difference.

I encourage you to revisit these exercises, practice them regularly, and integrate them into your daily life. Even just a few minutes each day can open the door to greater clarity, resilience, and peace. Remember, like any skill, the benefits of mindful breathing grow with consistency and patience.

As we move into the next chapter, we'll delve deeper into how breathing is intricately linked to trauma. We'll explore how the breath can guide us through healing past wounds and reclaiming a sense of safety and empowerment.

Chapter 5:

Understanding Trauma

Trauma is not what happens to you. Trauma is what happens inside you as a result of what happens to you. –Gabor Maté

We often encounter the word trauma in our daily lives. It is part of our vocabulary, and you will hear people use it in sentences to describe how they feel. But what is trauma? What qualifies an event as trauma? Is there a scientific explanation to define this? In this chapter, we will explore the answers to these questions and look into methods of addressing trauma.

We can define trauma as a distressing or disturbing experience that overwhelms your ability to cope with the world around you. As a result, you may have emotional, psychological, and physical responses that the trauma activates when suppressed and left unattended. Beyond all of this though, trauma affects the flow of energy from your core to all the other levels of your being. The light that emerges from your core carries with it the potential that you would otherwise use to orient yourself in life, and without it, you might feel off balance and stressed. This is why trauma often leaves you feeling helpless, vulnerable, and unable to process the situation in a way that allows you to move forward.

In my book, *The Divine Genogram*, I explore how trauma gets embedded within our Human Biofield. This accumulation of trauma is a leading cause for most diseases, both mental and physical. However, as you understand how trauma affects you in this chapter, the knowledge will empower you to transform painful situations to reclaim your inner flow and cosmic potential.

To understand how trauma impacts us, let's reflect in events that can cause it:

- Natural disasters: Earthquakes, wars, hurricanes, floods, and other catastrophic events can leave you feeling shocked and disoriented.

- Violence and abuse: Experiencing or witnessing physical, emotional, or sexual abuse, domestic violence, or other forms of interpersonal violence can have profound and lasting effects. This cause of trauma can happen pre-birth or during any stage of human development. If not addressed, it can deeply affect the nervous system. The stage at which the trauma occurred often imprints on the body's physiological responses and can manifest as specific types of contracted breath, as discussed in Chapter 4.

- Accidents and injuries: Car accidents, falls, and other serious injuries can cause both immediate and long-term trauma. Trauma to our physical bodies often reflects in the fifth level of our human biofield and chakra system which is the template for the physical body.

- Medical procedures: Undergoing invasive medical procedures, particularly without adequate preparation or understanding, can be traumatic.

- Sudden loss or grief: The unexpected death of a loved one, a breakup, or significant life changes can trigger intense emotional responses.

Regardless of the source, trauma can disrupt your sense of security, shatter your trust in the world, and leave you struggling to cope with the aftermath.

Based on the nature, duration, and depth of the experience, we can classify trauma into the following categories.

Types of Trauma

A single, isolated incident, like a car accident, a natural disaster, or a violent assault, usually activates this type of trauma. The effects of acute trauma can be intense but may not last long, depending on your ability to process and cope with the event. If you are involved in a serious car crash, you may feel shock, confusion, and anxiety. You may not even want to set foot in a car during the initial days after an accident. These feelings might resolve over time, especially with appropriate support and intervention.

Prolonged, repeated exposure to distressing events leads to chronic trauma. You may find yourself in situations where you feel trapped or unable to escape from your circumstances, such as ongoing domestic abuse, bullying, or prolonged exposure to war or violence.

Growing up during a wartime crisis or pandemic, for example, can result in chronic trauma due to repeated exposure to danger, loss, and grief. This constant exposure can lead to long-term psychological and emotional outcomes such as depression, anxiety, and difficulties in forming healthy relationships.

Next up we have multiple types of traumatic events that are experienced at the same time, such as sexual abuse, torture, or abandonment, which cause complex trauma. This may have undesirable effects on your mind, health, relationships, and work or school performance. You may struggle with trust issues, low self-esteem, and difficulties regulating your emotions. Seeking therapy and support from mental health professionals can help in processing and healing from complex trauma.

Furthermore, unresolved traumas from one generation can transfer to the next through behaviors, emotional patterns, epigenetics, and cultural or collective belief systems, leading to transgenerational trauma. This is another idea that we explore more in my other book, The Divine Genogram. You might experience this trauma through anxiety disorders, hypervigilance, repeated abusive patterns, or reactive responses to perceived abuse. It can also manifest as internalized toxic beliefs and judgments about yourself or others.

You can address these patterns through family systems therapy, couples counseling, or ancestral healing practices. These methods help you identify harmful patterns, adopt new strategies to transform behaviors, emotions, and thoughts, and reclaim a deeper sense of peace and well-being. The past doesn't need to define your present.

In my first book, *Blessings from a Thousand Generations*, I explore how the actions of our ancestors can have an effect on us today. In the book, I suggest an exercise where we look at the love bonds in the relationships of our ancestors to understand the patterns of negative and positive love bonds that might be transmitted from one generation to another. You incarnate into your family offering blessings that can heal the transgenerational patterns encoded in the DNA from both your parents. To your family, you bring blessings that can help remove the shroud over the light of your bloodline and heal these transgenerational patterns. I believe, in as much as we have transgenerational trauma, we also have the infinite wisdom and infinite love that can transfigure negative love bonds and foster positive love bonds for ourselves and the succeeding generations.

An example of transgenerational trauma was observed in a study among Holocaust survivors, where the parents' trauma altered their offspring's genes, increasing the risk of mental health issues like PTSD and depression even in the absence of a stressor (DeAngelis, 2023). This highlights the importance of addressing trauma, given its potential to be activated or transmitted genetically.

The transfer of trauma from one generation to another is not physical, and does not only happen when we grow up in the same environment as our ancestors. Rather, this is a process that happens when our cosmic core light, interpenetrates the hara dimension, enters the earth's plane, and enters the black velvet void of your mother's womb. It's during this process that we are connected to the DNA of our parents, and the bio-field of our ancestors. Trauma can be encoded and transmitted via the DNA, which is like a hall of records or gigabytes of ancestral history and origins.

Lastly, but just as important to understand is collective trauma. In the same way that we collect the past of our ancestors when we incarnate into this world, we also collect information about the community, country, or world we are born into. When something traumatic happens at a global scale, it is recorded in the Akashic field, and can affect anyone regardless of where they are from.

Because of this, a group of people who are not of the same ethnicity or culture can experience collective trauma, which can also precede generational trauma. Events that impact a country, region, or the entire world can cause collective trauma. An example is the recent COVID pandemic, which affected people from all walks of life, demonstrating how collective trauma can have widespread effects on diverse populations. Furthermore, we become desensitized to traumatic events, like war in other countries, that don't directly affect us. While we witness many atrocities on the news, repeated exposure to these events can have a collective impact. For some, this leads to numbness; for others, it results in heightened anxiety or overwhelming feelings of terror and grief.

DSM-5 Classification of Trauma

Another way to classify trauma is using the *Diagnostic and Statistical Manual of Mental Disorders, Fifth Edition* (DSM-5) (American Psychiatric Association, 2013). Many clinicians in the US follow this classification. We'll briefly look at the classification without going into detail.

Fist, we have Post-Traumatic Stress Disorder (PTSD), which often develops after a traumatic event, marked by recurring flashbacks, nightmares, and intense anxiety. These symptoms can feel overwhelming and persist for more than a month, disrupting daily life and emotional well-being.

When these symptoms emerge within the first month after the traumatic event, the condition is identified as Acute Stress Disorder (ASD). While ASD shares many features with PTSD, the key difference lies in timing. If the symptoms last beyond the initial month, the diagnosis may shift to PTSD, indicating a more chronic response to trauma.

Not all stress-related conditions create trauma. Adjustment disorders, for instance, occur in response to significant life changes or stressors. Symptoms typically appear within three months, causing difficulties in managing work, social interactions, or daily tasks. Fortunately, these symptoms often resolve within six months once the stressor or its aftermath has passed.

For children, the impact of neglect or unstable caregiving can lead to profound emotional challenges. Reactive Attachment Disorder (RAD), seen in children under five, stems from an inability to form secure attachments due to extreme neglect. These children may struggle to develop trust and rely on caregivers for emotional support.

In contrast, some children facing similar neglect develop Disinhibited Social Engagement Disorder (DSED). Rather than withdrawing, these children become overly familiar with strangers, displaying a lack of boundaries and inhibition. Both conditions highlight how early caregiving experiences can deeply shape a child's ability to connect with others.

Neurobiology of Trauma

We now understand trauma a little bit better and how it can affect our overall health, but you may still be wondering, What is the science behind it?

This section will concentrate on the scientific understanding of trauma's impact on the brain and body. We will examine some anatomy and physiology to understand the emotions experienced in trauma.

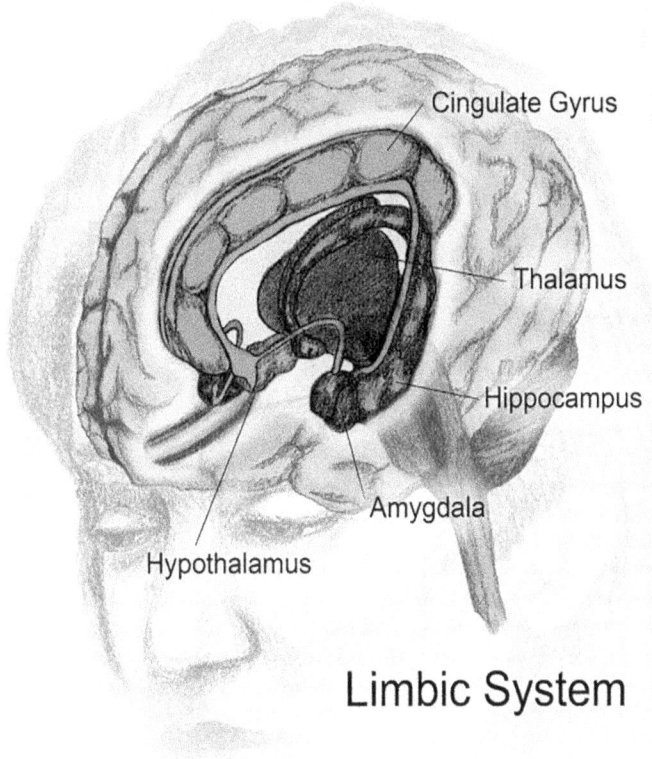

Limbic System

When a traumatic event occurs, the brain undergoes major changes as it processes the experience. The main areas affected include structures within the limbic system, such as the amygdala and hippocampus.

The limbic system is a complex network of brain structures that process emotions, form memories, and regulate automatic responses. It includes the amygdala, hippocampus, hypothalamus, and other interconnected structures. Unresolved trauma disrupts the limbic system's normal functioning, making it difficult for you to regulate your emotions and causing symptoms such as emotional numbness, mood swings, and difficulty experiencing pleasure or joy. Let's delve into the limbic system's most impacted areas.

Amygdala

The amygdala is an almond-shaped structure located on the temporal side of the brain and is responsible for processing emotions, particularly fear and pleasure. It is also known as the brain's fear center, as it is responsible for detecting threats and initiating the body's "fight-or-flight" response. Stressful or traumatic situations activate the amygdala, causing it to trigger the release of stress hormones such as cortisol and adrenaline. These hormones prepare your body to respond to the perceived danger.

If you have experienced unresolved trauma, your amygdala can become hyperactive, constantly scanning for threats and triggering anxiety or panic in situations that may not be dangerous. This heightened state of alertness can lead to hypervigilance, difficulty sleeping, irritability, and difficulty concentrating, which may affect your physical health.

Hippocampus

The hippocampus is also located in the temporal region of the brain and is responsible for forming and retrieving memories. Furthermore, it assists in integrating emotional and sensory information to create coherent memories of events. However, during a traumatic event, the high levels of stress hormones released in the body can impair the functioning of the hippocampus, causing it to change size and function. This makes it difficult to recall the details of the traumatic event accurately or have any memories of the situation. This can result in fragmented, intrusive memories or flashbacks, where you relive the traumatic experience as if it were happening in the present moment.

Stored Subconscious Trauma

You might go years without realizing you are carrying trauma that affects your thoughts, feelings, and actions. Subconscious trauma often arises from stressful experiences in your early life that you did not fully process emotionally and psychologically, but your brain integrated them into your conscious mind. Even though you may not be fully aware of these past traumas, they may continue to exert a powerful influence on your actions and health.

The limbic system is critical to the storage and manifestation of subconscious trauma. When you go through a distressing event, especially in your early years, the emotional intensity of the incident may overwhelm your brain's ability to fully understand and integrate it effectively. Your brain may store these traumatic experiences in a fragmented or distorted way. These unprocessed memories and emotions can become stuck in your subconscious, affecting your behavior and emotional responses without your conscious awareness.

Subconsciously held trauma in the limbic system can trigger a cascade of unconscious, unwanted repeated actions. You might find yourself avoiding certain situations or people, engaging in self-sabotaging behaviors, or experiencing unexplained fears or phobias. For example, suppose you experienced a traumatic event involving water as a child. In that case, your limbic system might store this experience as a threat, leading you to develop a fear of swimming or bathing even if you do not consciously remember the event.

Connection Between Breath and Trauma

Trauma affects more than just the limbic system; it can also affect breathing patterns, which can lead to anxiety and other mental health issues. Having discussed this, we will now delve into further scientific research to explore how trauma can impact your inspiration and expiration.

Studies show that people struggling with PTSD showed an increased respiratory rate and decreased tidal volume, which is the amount of air that moves in and out of the lungs during normal breathing, compared to people without trauma. An even higher number of individuals who self-reported having asthma and COPD also experienced traumatic events (Spitzer et al., 2011).

This scientific research supports that when we have trauma, we stop our breath and simultaneously our core light which prevents our authentic flow of creative energy from the life pulse. As early as the 1920s Wilhelm Reich and later other body-centered therapists, observed trauma as a series of prolonged contractions that would appear as body armoring and could be identified in the physical body posture. The survival responses of Fight, Flight, Freeze and Fawn can be seen in the physical body where the life pulse is held in prolonged stasis. Barbara Brennan, PhD. referred to these contracted states in Core light Healing as frozen time capsules, where trauma memories, beliefs, and emotions are stored in the human energy consciousness field and physical body. The contraction of the core also shows up in our physical posture, mostly in our breathing patterns. When we are afraid, we often freeze, flee, or fight. Trauma is most associated with the freeze response, where we hold our breath and tighten our bodies instead of being open and breathing in the much-needed oxygen.

Another study observed that people with PTSD showed reduced respiratory sinus arrhythmia (RSA) (Campbell et al., 2019). RSA is the normal change in your heart rate that happens during the breathing cycle. Your heart rate increases a little when you breathe in. When you exhale, it gradually decreases. However, due to unresolved trauma, your RSA may decrease. The same study revealed that a reduced RSA is linked to a decrease in physiological arousal, which could potentially lead to hypervigilance and anxiety. It also increases the risk of developing cardiovascular diseases such as hypertension and heart disease.

Emotional Suppression

Emotional suppression is the intentional act of avoiding feeling or expressing emotions. Unlike subconscious trauma, you will be aware of your feelings, but you will choose to ignore them as a coping mechanism. This approach can help in the short term, but it can also cause unresolved trauma and make healing more difficult. Cultural and societal conventions that prohibit the expression of specific emotions also play a role in this learned behavior, which develops during childhood. These staggering emotions can persist at a subconscious level, affecting your behavior and relationships.

Concerning trauma, unprocessed emotions can cause you to struggle to acknowledge and work through the pain and fear associated with your trauma. This avoidance can lead to a lack of closure and hinder the processing of your experience.

In addition, it may exacerbate the symptoms of trauma, including flashbacks, nightmares, anxiety, and depression. Furthermore, research has shown that suppressing emotions can lead to increased stress levels, weakened immune function, and a higher risk of developing chronic health conditions (Segerstrom & Miller, 2004). Moreover, your inability to express your emotions openly may lead to struggles with effective communication with others, hindering your chances of forming meaningful connections. This can lead to feelings of isolation, loneliness, and detachment from others, making it difficult to heal the trauma you carry.

How Breathwork Addresses Trauma

Going through day-to-day life with trauma can be a heavy burden for you psychologically, physically, and spiritually. It is even worse if you are carrying trauma that you are not aware of. The positive news is that several approaches can kick-start your journey to healing trauma. We are going to look into the behind-the-scenes science of how breathwork can help you heal from trauma. We'll also include some insightful exercises and other trauma management methods that you can start using today.

We have discussed how trauma can activate the sympathetic nervous system, which helps us be alert to dangerous situations. Normally, dangerous situations stimulate this system, but unresolved trauma can lead to hyper-alertness and anxiety, even in the absence of danger. In previous chapters, we also briefly mentioned how breathwork can activate the parasympathetic nervous system, which aids in counteracting the sympathetic effects of the fight-or-flight response. The parasympathetic nervous system is often activated through slow, deep breathing, particularly diaphragmatic breathing, which shifts the body from a state of hyperarousal to one of relaxation and recovery.

The science behind this is that deep diaphragmatic breathing increases the activity of the vagus nerve, the part of the parasympathetic nervous system that connects your brain to the body. The vagus nerve communicates with the brain via the gut–brain axis, which is a two-way communication system of nerves between your brain and gut. As a result, this influences your heart rate, digestion, and stress responses. Activation of the vagus nerve triggers the release of acetylcholine, a key neurotransmitter. This chemical aids in reducing heart rate and lowering blood pressure, promoting a state of calm and relaxation. This indicates that breathwork could potentially stabilize the autonomic nervous system, thereby reducing the chronic stress reaction associated with unresolved trauma.

Hypothalamic–Pituitary–Adrenal Axis Regulation

The hypothalamic–pituitary–adrenal (HPA) axis is responsible for your body's response to stress, regulating cortisol levels and other hormones. Chronic stress or trauma can disrupt this system due to its prolonged activation, leading to negative health effects such as anxiety and depression.

According to a study, practicing high ventilation breathwork reduces cortisol levels by modulating the activity of the HPA axis (Fincham et al., 2023). Another study showed that slowing your breathing rate helps reduce stress markers in your body by reducing the secretion of corticotropin-releasing hormone (CRH), which leads to lower levels of adrenocorticotropic hormone (ACTH) and cortisol, resulting in a lower physiological stress response (Dillard et al., 2023).

Neural Modulation and Emotional Regulation

Recall the limbic system and its role in processing trauma and storing emotional memories. Breathing exercises reduce the amygdala's hyperactivity, which is overactive in untreated trauma. This reduction is possible because breathwork increases prefrontal cortex function, a part of the brain responsible for higher cognitive functions such as decision-making and emotion regulation. This interaction allows for better control over fear and stress responses, reducing the intensity of traumatic memories.

Improving Neuroplasticity

Neuroplasticity is the brain's ability to service itself by forming new neural connections. This helps rewire the brain, which can be beneficial if you want to recover from a traumatic event as it facilitates the creation of new pathways that can support healing and recovery.

Your brain can form new neural pathways that promote emotional resilience and recovery through repeated breathwork practice. A study reported that regular breathing exercises increased gamma-aminobutyric acid (GABA) levels in the brain; this neurotransmitter helps inhibit neural activity, reducing symptoms of anxiety and emotional regulation in trauma recovery (Brenner, 2019). Another study revealed that after 12 weeks of breathwork and yoga, participants who had major depressive disorders showed improved mood and decreased symptoms of depression (Streeter et al., 2020). This evidence shows how breathwork aids in immediate stress reduction and long-term emotional healing.

Healing Subconscious Trauma

Addressing subconscious trauma requires a comprehensive approach that integrates both conscious and unconscious processing. Several techniques help to bring subconscious trauma to the surface, such as breathwork, Brennan energetic time capsule healing, body-centered psychotherapy, emotional freedom technique (EFT), psychotherapy, and mindfulness. With the help of a trained specialist, these practices can aid you in processing and recovering from traumatic memories. Let's explore these methods.

Brennan Time Capsule Healing

In the Brennan Method, Time Capsule Healing focuses on releasing old emotional wounds trapped in your body's energy field. When you go through a traumatic experience, it can leave an energetic time capsule in your energy. Time capsules are pockets of trapped energy within your body's energy field that hold unresolved emotions, pain, or memories from the time the trauma occurred.

Using this healing method, a trained Brennan healer works with your energy field to reveal these time capsules, help release the stuck emotions, and free your core light. Release of the capsules enables your body and mind to heal from the past, achieve greater balance, and break free from the emotional burden you've been carrying.

Body-Centered Psychotherapy

In previous chapters, we covered the origin of this therapeutic technique, so we won't go into detail here. Bioenergetic therapy is a body-based therapy that can help address the physical and emotional consequences of trauma stored deep within your subconscious mind. If you recall, the fundamental principle of this therapy is the connection between the mind and body, where emotional traumas stored in the body can lead to physical blockages or tensions. A trained instructor will help you with some bioenergetic exercises that involve grounding techniques, deep breathing, and expressive movements to encourage the release of suppressed emotions.

Studies have shown that body-centered therapy is more cited in recent times than it has ever been, and that people who engage in bioenergetic exercises experience a reduction in anxiety, depression, and PTSD symptoms. This shows its effectiveness in both subconscious and conscious trauma recovery (Invitto & Moselli, 2024).

Body-based therapy focuses on your body's natural ability to heal from trauma by addressing the physical sensations associated with traumatic events. During your somatic experience, your instructor will guide you to become attuned to the subtle bodily sensations associated with trauma, such as tightness, heat, or tingling. They will do so in a mindful and carefully controlled environment. This will help your body's innate fight, flight, or freeze responses to complete the reaction disrupted during the traumatic event. The gradual adjustment of traumatic sensations allows your brain to discharge the energy associated with the trauma, leading to a sense of relief and giving you a brand new start.

Emotional Freedom Techniques (EFT)

Also known as tapping, EFT is a therapeutic method that combines elements of cognitive therapy with physical tapping on specific acupressure points on the body. These points are referred to as meridians. Traditional Chinese medicine uses meridians, which are energy pathways that transport vital energy throughout the body. Tapping these points calms the nervous system, helping you release emotional stress and reframe negative thoughts associated with trauma.

Psychotherapy

Different types of psychotherapy treatment can assist in identifying and modifying the troubling behaviors and patterns associated with mental health. Let's briefly look into the various types:

- Cognitive behavioral therapy (CBT): CBT is a structured, goal-oriented therapeutic approach that identifies and modifies negative thought patterns and behaviors. It is effective in addressing trauma by aiding you to identify and reframe unproductive beliefs associated with traumatic experiences.

- Eye movement desensitization and reprocessing (EMDR): EMDR is a specialized therapy that involves bilateral stimulation, like eye movements or tapping, to assist the brain in processing and integrating traumatic memories. This technique aims to lessen the emotional distress linked to traumatic memories and enhance overall psychological well-being.

- Dialectical behavior therapy (DBT): Originally used to treat borderline personality disorder, DBT combines cognitive behavioral techniques with mindfulness practices. It can help you regulate emotions and develop positive coping skills and interpersonal effectiveness, making it a valuable tool for trauma recovery.

Strategies for Emotional Suppression

Emotional suppression can feel like a natural response to

overwhelming situations, but holding emotions inside often creates more harm than good. When emotions like anger, sadness, or fear are buried, they don't disappear—they linger, affecting mental and physical health in subtle but powerful ways. Suppression can lead to heightened stress, anxiety, and even physical symptoms like chronic pain or fatigue, as the body and mind struggle to carry unresolved emotional weight.

As we mentioned earlier, when there is trauma at any point in your life, it goes and blocks the flow of light from your core. Trauma that you are actively working to overcome might be less dangerous than the trauma that you suppress and harbor in your energy system. In this section, we are going to focus on individual approaches that can help you reduce the intensity of your pain and promote healing.

Journaling

Sometimes, all roads lead back to pen and paper; the best way to express yourself is by writing down your thoughts and feelings on paper. In doing so, you may become aware of the emotions you tend to avoid and gain the courage to confront the reasons behind your avoidance. This way, you will be free to express yourself in a safe and private space.

You can dedicate 10–20 minutes each day to journaling. Feel your emotions, and allow them to guide you without blocking them. You can also couple journaling with mindfulness to get even better results. Combining journaling and mindful breathing methods can help unblock different types of trauma held deep within the body. Exploring literature such as the Hindu-Yogi Science of Breath (Ramacharaka, 2013/1903) or other literature on somatic healing can guide you through some practical exercises. When paired with mindfulness practices, journaling aids in physical release and brings unconscious thoughts and feelings to the surface, giving you time to process them without bias.

Let's explore how to make journaling and breathwork more effective in your life.

1. As with most of the exercises we have gone over in this book, start by setting aside a calm and distraction-free area where you can write and practice mindfulness. Having a specific space helps condition your mind to associate that area with reflection and healing.

2. Begin your journaling session by sitting quietly for 3–5 minutes and focusing on your breath—the cosmic breath flowing through you. Inhale deeply through your nose for a count of four, hold for four, and exhale slowly for six seconds. This will help ground you and open your mind to introspection.

3. Before writing, think about what you want to explore. It could be a specific emotion, a recent experience, or simply uncovering hidden thoughts. Saying your intention aloud or silently to yourself creates a sense of purpose.

4. Write freely and without judgment. Spend 10–20 minutes journaling, allowing your thoughts and feelings to flow naturally. Don't worry about grammar or structure; focus on expressing yourself authentically. If you're unsure where to start, you can write prompts such as "What am I feeling right now?" or "What am I avoiding and why?"

5. After journaling, try some of the breathwork practices outlined in this book.

6. Once your meditation session is complete, take a moment to sit quietly and reflect on what surfaced during the journaling session. Close your eyes and visualize releasing any lingering tension or negativity, creating space for peace and clarity.

7. Review your progress weekly by revisiting your journal entries. Look for patterns or insights about your emotional or intellectual reactions.. This practice helps you track your emotional journey and highlights areas for further exploration.

Through combining these practices, you create a powerful routine that nurtures emotional release, self-discovery, and holistic healing.

Creativity

You don't have to be talented in the arts, but using your creativity as a way to express yourself can help process suppressed emotions. Instead of shutting your feelings down, try engaging in activities such as painting, drawing, or listening to music that reflects your feelings. This will serve as a nonverbal outlet for expressing your emotions.

Creativity and emotional expression are deeply intertwined because creativity provides a non-linear, intuitive pathway to explore and process feelings that might otherwise remain unacknowledged. While words can sometimes feel limiting or inaccessible—especially when dealing with complex or deeply rooted emotions—creative outlets offer freedom. They allow you to express emotions in ways that bypass logical thinking and reach deeper parts of your psyche.

Art, music, writing, and other creative endeavors engage the brain's right hemisphere, which is associated with intuition, imagination, and emotional processing. By activating this part of the brain, creativity allows you to access emotions you may not consciously recognize or articulate. In doing this, creativity bridges the gap between internal experiences and external expression. When you create, you externalize what's happening inside you, giving those feelings a tangible form. This process can bring clarity to emotions that feel overwhelming or chaotic. Writing a poem, composing music, or even crafting something physical can help transform abstract emotions into something concrete and manageable. It can also help you identify patterns in your feelings, offering a new perspective on your emotional landscape.

Creativity can also evoke a sense of liberation and empowerment. Expressing emotions through art or music helps you regain a sense of control over them. Rather than feeling trapped or overwhelmed, you take an active role in channeling those feelings into something meaningful and beautiful. This process not only alleviates emotional tension but can also enhance your resilience, equipping you to face future challenges with a greater sense of confidence and inner peace.

Professional Support

Learning to express emotions openly is an integral part of addressing emotional suppression. Doing this in a safe and supportive environment can help you release suppressed emotions and improve your emotional regulation. You can practice this with a trusted friend, family member, or therapist.

Working with a Brennan healer, therapist, or bodyworker who specializes in trauma and emotional suppression can help you process and understand the root causes of your emotional suppression. They can provide guidance and tools to help you healthily deal with your emotions.

As you continue your journey through trauma recovery, healing your mind and body is a crucial step toward reaping the fullest benefits of life. Now, we are going to turn our attention to understanding character analysis, core quality traits, and how hidden trauma may shape your behavior and emotions.

Chapter 6:

Character Analysis and Personality Patterns

Tension is a habit. Relaxing is a habit. Bad habits can be broken, good habits formed. –William James

Sigmund Freud, the founding father of psychoanalysis, introduced the concept of character analysis in the late 19th century. Freud's theories focused on the unconscious mind, how our early childhood experiences may shape our personalities, and the role of trauma in shaping our character. The theories were later published in this book *The Interpretation of Dreams* (Freud, 1999). He theorized that these experiences from our childhood persist into adulthood, influencing our behavior and personality. He further explored how the mind contains structures such as the id, ego, and superego and how unresolved conflicts within these structures could manifest as neuroses or other psychological disturbances.

Later, Freud's student Wilhelm Reich advanced these theories further by recognizing that there is a connection between the body and the psyche. In his book, *Character Analysis,* originally published as *Charakteranalyse* in 1933, Reich (2003), developed the concept of character armor, which we briefly talked about in Chapter 4. Character armor describes the habitual physical and emotional tensions that we develop as defenses against psychological pain. These tensions are often the result of our repressed emotions, assumptions, and unresolved childhood trauma. Reich's theories pioneered the field of body centered psychotherapy, breathwork, and left a legacy of various techniques to free the flow of energy in the body.

Building on the work of Reich, who also served as his mentor, Alexander Lowen along with John Pierrakos founded the field of bioenergetics. This was a combination of psychotherapy with physical exercises intended to release chronic muscular tensions that restrict emotional expression (Lowen, 2012). They noted that the body reflects the personality pattern and that working directly with the body can help heal psychological trauma. This method emphasized the importance of understanding the physical manifestations of character defenses and using them to achieve deeper emotional healing.

John Pierrakos expanded on these theories by veering away from Lowen to focus on the energy at the core of one's being, which becomes contracted within these defensive patterns. Their work is an important intersection for energy healing and our understanding of character analysis, especially with books like *Core Energetics* (Pierrakos, 1987).

Barbara Brennan is another worthy mention in the evolution of character analysis. Having studied bioenergetics in the early 1970s with both Alexander Lowen and John Pierrakos, she later became a core energetics therapist, combining character analysis with the dynamics of the human energy field. She introduced these concepts to the public in her groundbreaking book, *Hands of Light*, (Brennan, 1990), while also establishing a school that focuses on the five personality patterns and a systematic approach to the human energy consciousness system—The Barbara Brennan School of Healing.

In her second book, *Light Emerging, Brennan* (1993) further illustrated the energetic interactions between different personality patterns and provided guidance on how to offer healing responses for yourself and others to reestablish healthy relationships. She further redefined each personality pattern by using the four dimensions of human existence, which are the physical, auric, hara, and core star dimensions. Courageously, Brennan introduced the concept of the four dimensions of humankind, later renamed to the human energy consciousness system to describe the concept of one's being. The first of these dimensions is the core of one's being arising from a core star—a singularity or point of light emerging from deep within oneself.

The next dimension or level would relate to intentionality and is what Japanese Martial Artists refer to as the Hara. The third level is the human energy consciousness field that includes the seven levels and seven chakras. The physical body is what we see as denser vibrating consciousness and energy. Brennan's scientific analysis of the chakra system and levels of the field identifies our physical, emotional, psychological, relational and spiritual memories. Her work led to the revolutionary concept of cosmic breath, which posits that our breath and pranic energy emerge from deep within the universe and are holographically connected throughout our human energy consciousness system (HECS).

One distinction between Brennan and her predecessors is her reversal of the order of character defenses, placing masochism during the rapprochement stage of toddlerhood (9 months to 2 1/2 years) and aggressive at the fourth stage (2 1/2 to 4 years), where a child's loyalty to both parents may be compromised, setting up a dynamic with the same-sex parent. Her work helped bridge traditional psychotherapy and holistic healing, offering a broad foundation for understanding and transforming personality patterns through energy dynamics.

In 1990, other notable contributors were Ronald Robbins, who, in Rhythmic Integration, reframed all the character defenses from the perspective of the creative life pulse of the universe (Robbins, 1990). Similar to Brennan, Robbins extends beyond character defenses to recapture the true potential of each developmental stage. Because of his perspective, Robbins chose to rename the character defenses to reflect the positive aspects: Dreamer,

Creator, Communicator, Inspirer, Solidifier, and Achiever.

In addition, Steven Kessler's book *The Five Personality Patterns* reframes the context of personality patterns, whose labels were rooted in pathology, as survival-based instincts (Kessler & Chrisman, 2015). Instead of Schizoid, Kessler preferred to rename character patterns as "Leaving", the Oral as Merging, Masochism as Endurer, Psychopathy as Aggressive and Rigid as Achiever. Rather than focusing on pathology he focused on both the strengths and weaknesses of each pattern and the impact on relationships with others.

In the evolution of my work, I prefer to refer to these patterns as creative solutions to navigating being human. This requires a paradigm shift in our concept of being a physical being towards understanding our cosmic origins and our human energy consciousness system (HECS). The core energy, or life pulse of all human beings follows the rhythm of the cosmos and breath. The five personality patterns described by Kessler refer to the life pulse in a prolonged contracted state due to adaptation to repeated stimuli. Just as Reich had described these same patterns in the early 1930's and focused primarily on breathwork to unfreeze the armoring appearing in the physical body. This book serves as a practical guide that integrates evolution of breathwork in body-centered psychotherapy and spiritual practices.

To understand these core qualities and five personality patterns we need to explore the concept of the life pulse. Later in this chapter, I describe the five core quality traits as Creative, Expressive, Integrative, Expansive and Achievement. These follow the natural movement and wave of the life pulse through the incarnation process. Then we will explore the different patterns that occur when there are prolonged contracted states. Cosmic breath refers to reclaiming our natural flow and releasing the contracted patterns.

To understand these core qualities and character analysis defenses, we will first discuss the concept of the life pulse.

The Life Pulse

Before we begin, let's take a moment and breathe. I want you to think of a time when you were in a positive mood and experiencing life's joy, whether in creativity or moments of peace within yourself. Your life pulse is flowing now, allowing you to experience the best of life.

Take another breath. I invite you to think of other moments when life seemed to stand still. You may notice that you no longer find joy in things you like. You might feel disconnected from yourself, experiencing tension in your body, and think that nothing is going your way. Even on days you thought would be better, this feeling of stuckness may persist. While you might choose to ignore this feeling, it is a signal from your body, a sign that the natural flow of energy from your life pulse has become blocked. This block disrupts your flow of creativity, expression, and connection with others.

At each stage of life, trauma can impact the flow of life energy which forms our personality and shapes our character. Understanding how our mind forms ideas, concepts and ideas throughout different stages in childhood can help us identify false assumptions that currently impact our behavior today. Understanding how our life pulse is regulated from our first breath of life into our last breath is essential to our healing process. What happens to you, especially during incarnation up to about five years, influences how your life pulse—cosmic breath—will react. The life pulse will either expand when the environment is safe, or contract when it meets obstacles.

Interruptions to this flow, whether brought on by trauma, stress, or unresolved emotional pain, can interfere with the life pulse. Situations like birth trauma or the need to separate a newborn from the mother due to medical emergencies, such as transporting them to neonatal care or placing them in an incubator, can impact the life pulse's flow. While such interventions are life-saving, it's important to be aware that they may still create energetic imbalances, affecting the newborn's breath, emotional connection, and long-term well-being. This shows the importance of a trauma-free pregnancy and birth in establishing a healthy life pulse flow in a child.

Within this creative wave you have the potential to heal and reclaim the divine flow from within. Your full creative potential emerges from the unmanifest world into the manifest world as the cycle of creation completes each phase. You become unified with creation itself and allow its potential to flow through you, manifesting your dreams and fulfilling your destiny. Every newborn that is welcomed into a safe and trusting environment, records these experiences deep within the limbic system. In addition, these first experiences become recorded beyond the physicality of the limbic system, they are encoded within the human energy consciousness system in a holographic way setting the stage for healthy development and expression of core qualities and traits.

When the life pulse flows smoothly through these phases, experience your full cosmic potential, co-creating healthy relationships, and discovering your sense of purpose. Remember, everything you need to have a successful life is already within you nested within your core. As you allow the flow from your core essence, you bring the blessings that are only potential within you to manifestation. A child born into welcoming circumstances develops an instinct of safety and trust in their limbic system, setting the stage for healthy development and expression of core quality traits later in life.

The life pulse is energy that flows through all forms of life in a rhythmic pattern that facilitates growth, transformation, and creation. It is the primary current that drives the body, mind, and spirit, determining how we interact with life and express our authentic selves. The life pulse flows through the cosmic principles of expansion, stasis, contraction, and stasis. This flow of energy starts from within and spreads outward into the surrounding world, bringing out creativity and connection. Let's take a closer look at the principles of the flow of the life pulse.

Expansion and Stasis

During the expansion phase, the life pulse moves outward, radiating from within. This phase represents the creative wave, when ideas, emotions, and life energy come out of you. You may think of these as peak moments. This phase is a time of growth, expansion, and reaching out to the world.

The human phases begin at conception when the sperm and egg unite, promoting the process of cellular division. This division is an explosion of the expansion phase, marking the activation of the life pulse, which continues through the development of the fetus, nurturing the creative abilities of the incoming soul energy within the sacred container of the mother's womb.

As the life pulse reaches its peak of expansion, it moves into stasis, which is a moment of stillness where the energy rests, allowing stabilization. At this moment, everything seems to pause, but beneath the surface, the energy is gathering itself, ready for the next phase of movement. When the expansion phase reaches its full potential activating DNA and Cellular memory, it reverses order in the stasis phase, and prepares to bring information from the expansion into a contraction phase. The natural rhythm in life can be seen everywhere from the waves of an ocean to the ripples in a pond. Let's explore the contraction phase.

Contraction and Stasis

Following stasis, there is contraction, which is the inward pull of energy that is returning to the core. While expansion is about reaching outward, contraction is about returning inward to process and transform what you have experienced. It is a time of self-reflection, containment, and restoration. This contraction allows the body and mind to heal, recuperate, and make sense of the outward experiences.

We can link the contraction phase to birth, where the baby's body contracts before its first breath, preparing itself for life beyond the womb. The birth process itself is a manifestation of this life pulse, involving stages of expansion, stasis, and now contraction.

The life pulse again enters a phase of stasis, a second moment of stillness. During this time, the energy fully integrates before beginning the cycle again. This stage is important as it gives you space to fully process emotions and experiences from the previous phases. This pause is important because it helps to maintain a healthy, continuous flow of the life pulse. Let us consider the above more closely in the next section.

The Life Pulse in Flow

The table on the next page identifies personality patterns that are used in body centered psychotherapy. These patterns identify several types of body armoring and how a prolonged contraction of the life pulse is held in the physical body. The life pulse in flow can be seen across the top of the chart as creative, expressive, integrative, expansive, creative. This wave represents the creative life force entering the earth plane from the unmanifest world, expressing itself, integrating into the physical plane of existence, expanding into the creative manifest world.

When you read the chart vertically, you will notice how the life pulse responds or reacts when contacted at a certain stage of development. The life pulse in a chronic contracted state appears as body armoring. The cosmic breath of life becomes held in different areas, upper chest or thoracic area, the diaphragm area, or lower abdomen. These contractions are seen in different personality patterns such as leaving, collapsing, merging, withdrawing, aggressiveness, or containment. Use the chart

The Life Pulse in Flow

Life Pulse in Flow	Creative Wave	Expressive Wave	Integrative Wave	Expansive: Inspired Wave	Creative: Achievement Wave
Life Pulse in contraction	Leaving	Collapsed	Withheld	Aggressive	Contained
Character defense	Schizoid	Oral	Masochism	Psychopathy	Rigid
Age	Pre Birth, birth	0–1.5 months	1.5–36 months	3–4.5 years	4.5–5 years
Body armor and blocks	Weak and disjointed with blah-block and leaks	Upper chest with depletion	Compaction and blah block well-rounded	Chest and hips with mesh compaction	Contained mesh and plate armor with stillness
Breath wave	Diaphragm is pushed up into the upper chest, and energy leaves through the head	Diaphragm is pushed up with the upper chest collapsed, and waves contracted	Slow, shallow breath, wave held inside	Abdomen frozen, wave pushed from diaphragm into upper chest	Shallow, held at periphery
Fear	Fear of living in a physical body and going crazy.	Fear of abandonment, rejection, deprivation, and not having enough of anything.	Fear of being overwhelmed and losing control	Betrayal: Fear of chaos and losing control	Imperfection: Fear of being taken advantage of and not getting what one needs
Reactive response	Leaves	Merges	Hides Self	Control/Power	Appropriate
Gifts	Artistic, visual	Communicates, teaches	Integrator, loyal	Inspires, protects	Achiever

to help you identify what type of patterns that may impact the creative flow of your life pulse.

The Five Personality Patterns

From birth, your experiences, especially those involving your primary caregivers, shape your character and personality in different ways. According to attachment theory, the quality of a child's early attachment or bond with their caregiver significantly influences their emotional and psychological development. This theory further explains that secure bonds provide a foundation for healthy emotional regulation and resilience, while insecure attachments can lead to patterns of anxiety, avoidance, or disorganized behavior (Cherry, 2023).

In *The Divine Genogram*, I review the incarnation process, exploring how we emerged from the black velvet void and the infinite intelligent universe as light into physical cosmic beings. The book illuminates a scientific paradigm shift that suggests we are holographically and interdimensionally interwoven into the matrix of the infinite universe. Before incarnation, we are light that is emerging from the black velvet void of the universe into the black velvet void of our mother's womb. We interpenetrate our divine spark and unite with the gestation process of our parents' cells dividing. The DNA code is unlocked and engaged in the selection process via the frequencies transmitting from your intention to incarnate and the human energy consciousness field and chakra system.

You begin to emerge from the unmanifest world into the manifest world becoming a human being. Your full awakened consciousness rests within the matrix of your family mind field and the collective human mind fields within the matrix of the earth. Although we are still held within a universal awareness within the holographic matrix of these fields, our human mind hasn't developed until our chakra system and our human biofield goes through several developmental stages from before birth into adulthood and beyond.

Upon incarnating into the physical realm of the earth, our soul and core light engage with different experiences from pleasure to the atrocities of war and trauma. The energetic frequencies either are welcoming and harmonizing or transmit unwelcoming, harsh and disharmonious energy. At each stage of development, the incoming soul adapts and achieves each milestone, from expressing one's needs, likes and dislikes from infancy to learning to sit, crawl and walk into toddler stage. During these phases, our personality traits are formed around the principles of the life pulse.

Each phase of the life pulse goes through the expansion stasis, contraction, stasis and can flow freely or engage in a prolonged contraction. The phases that impact the formation of our personality traits are creative, expressive, to integrative, to expansion, and creative/achievement. As stated, the full wave of the life pulse- core light continues to interact with the parents and the environment navigating and completing each developmental stage from birth to transition from the manifest world to the unmanifest world.

Any interruption to the flow of the life pulse at any developmental stage causes a contraction in the life force and later can be seen and described as personality patterns. These patterns become embedded into the physical body as armoring and can be seen in the body posture. Similar to one of your favorite sweaters where you snag and pull a piece of the yarn and it changes shape due to the pulled yarn. Imagine your core light interwoven into the very fabric of your being and your energy field has threads holographically interwoven through your physical body. When one of the threads contracts or is pulled inwards it will impact the shape of the physical body.

When we are incarnating in this physical realm, we might hesitate to fully bring out light into the world. This is very prevalent when we sense the pain and the trauma that surround the field we are incarnating into. This continues as we are growing up, we may have encountered different challenges and struggles that contributed to the formation of our personality pattern. These challenges may have included family dynamics, social interactions, and cultural influences. These situations led to the development of defense mechanisms to cope with the challenges you faced. At the time, the reactions are not really defense mechanisms, but rather natural responses to the environment we are assimilating to. These responses may have been imprinted into your human energy consciousness field and are reflected in your personality and body structure.

Creative Life Pulse in Contraction
Leaving Pattern

The first personality pattern is leaving, also referred to as creative. This happens between pregnancy and birth most of the time. As I highlight in *The Divine Genogram*, it is during these stages in incarnation that our soul is still able to move back and forth between the new forming physical reality, and the higher dimension from which we come.

During the incarnation process, the two options presented are to react or respond as our light interpenetrates the developing embryo. We either continue the interpenetration into the physical plane within our mother's womb or we react by leaving and moving back into the astral plane. Brennan refers to this stage as being between two worlds. When entering the earth plane, if the soul is met by harsh or chaotic energy it contracts and pulls away because of the incoherent frequency.

According to Brenan (1990):

> "The natural energetic defense used against this trauma at this stage of life is simply to draw back into the spirit world from which the soul is coming. The defense is developed and used for this type of personality pattern until it is very easy for the person simply to withdraw into someplace "away," which is into the spirit world (pg.110)."

If you have the leaving pattern, then you often remove yourself from situations that make you feel afraid. While in most cases the 'leaving' might be physically moving from a space, or avoiding looking at something, it can also be mentally and spiritually redirecting energy from the situation to something else. Someone who has a leaving pattern can be at a party enjoying with everyone else, but a simple thought, or offence can pull them away from the party. Even though physically they might still be present, their intention, thoughts, spirit and mind would be somewhere else. This reaction can be likened to the avoidance attachment style, which primarily actively avoids anything that brings anxiety or fear.

When such a pattern has been repeated throughout the developmental stages, the person will end up sharpening the gift of openness and creativity through it. All creative ideas flow to us from the infinite universe, and we should open ourselves in submission to our intention to receive these creative ideas. Since the person who is leaving can more easily leave the world and bring their mind and subconscious to the attention of the potential that is within the infinite universe, they have better access to creative and novel ideas.

In "Ye! An Afrobeats Musical" there is a famous line; "Name one genius that ain't crazy". This identifies how creativity emerges from the depths of some of our most inspirational scientists and artists, like Nicola Tesla, Mozart, Beethoven and Picasso to name a few. The creative process is one that requires a person to expand beyond the limitations of this world and to be inspired by unlimited potentialities. In his book, *Rhythmic Integration*, Robbins identified the creative potential and originality inherent in those who struggle with the leaving pattern (Robbins 1990). He acknowledges their creative imagination, insights and brilliant minds as an inherent gift allowing direct access to the higher realms. From these realms our creativity, innovative ideas, and breakthroughs are discovered. Robbin's renamed the schizoid term of this character type to the creator-dreamer.

Expressive Life Pulse in Contraction Collapsed Pattern

The hallmark of birth to around 18 months of age, occurs upon the first breath of incarnation. As the newborn first cries of expression arise from the moving through the life pulse of expansion-stasis, contraction-stasis from the mother womb into the world. The first breath of life, breathing on one's own starts the individuation process from being merged with the mother. I am here. The infant now is in the sea of life. The soul seeks to orient to this new place and starts the bonding and process of attachment.

The child learns to merge their energy with the primary caregiver to create a connection. They are in a process of learning from the first sounds of communication and then a response from the parents. The response encourages more expressiveness and communication. This process of engagement creates an internal sense of excitement and pleasure or the opposite sense of loss and disappointment when the expressiveness isn't met or reciprocated. Each of these phases of expressiveness are developmentally hardwired into the deep limbic system and are interwoven into the stages of separation and individuation from a symbiotic merged state of oneness into the first stages of individuation to fulfill one's needs, to a sense of autonomy.

As this process continues the infant internalizes the experiences of individuation through the expression of fulfilling one's needs, searching for the mother's breast when hungry, to lifting one's head and eventually crawling and standing.

The infant moves from the sensorimotor stage where everything is explored through the mouth and expression. The life pulse, expands with expression to meet one's needs is either met with satisfaction or loss, then moves into stasis to integrate the experience and then contracts with that information, and moves into stasis again. Each aspect of the life pulse either supports the needs of the infants or rejects it. The internalized sense of loss can result in an energetic collapse. This experience becomes mapped into the unconscious as a preverbal experience. The infant is learning to adapt and navigate to being human by discovering and expressing their basic needs provided attachment to the parents or caregivers.

One example, can happen when the mother or caregiver is unavailable or unattentive to the cries or the infant. Perhaps leaving the infant in the crib crying too long which eventually lends itself to the collapsing pattern. Out of exhaustion the infant collapses from frustration and loss of energy. These experiences again are mapped into the unconsciousness as preverbal experiences.

The preverbal conclusions rest just beneath consciousness and form as a collapsing rather than merging pattern. Both patterns tend to orient around a belief that " I cannot get my needs met" I am not enough. I need someone to do it for me." The merging pattern arises when the parent is unattentive and the infant learns to adapt by trying to reach the parent via sounds. Unconsciously the infant learns to mirror or respond to the parent rather than the parent learning to mirror and respond to the infant. You may see these patterns expressed in the next stage.

When this persists into adulthood, the person merges with the other, often suppressing one's needs while accommodating the other's needs. When there are differences in how the expressive person sees the world and how another person does, the expressive is often willing to forgo their own experiences to make the other person happy. In most situations, the merging type is always looking outward, trying to see whose life they can improve. The merging pattern can often be self-sacrificing, putting the needs of others ahead of their own excessively.

On the other hand, when this has been practiced subconsciously for a long time, it becomes a gift for the individual. People with this pattern, usually are highly intelligent, emotionally and socially intelligent, and can understand the needs of others before they share. They are great with inclusiveness within an organization and they are empathic and focused on the interconnections between people.

Challenges related to nurturing and dependence, particularly during the first nine months of life, contribute to the development of this personality pattern. The person may shift from collapsing pattern, to merging pattern, to overcompensating pattern, often feeling defeated and looking for outside support. This body expresses this pattern as physically thin and fragile. On an emotional level, the person may feel needy, clingy.

Robbins recognized the innate gift of this personality pattern as nurturing. From experiencing a lack of nurturing during this developmental stage, the person innately understands the needs of others, and when the expressive energy flows freely they are great communicators, teachers and leaders. On the other hand, when the person collapses you may experience their energy draining and their words are hard to hear drawing you in as if you are being sucked into taking care of them. Robbins sees them as transforming dependency into a powerful nurturing presence. Let's explore the transition from this stage to the next.

Integrative Life Pulse in Contraction Withheld Pattern

During the toddler phase, the child moves out into the world, learning how to integrate oneself as a separate person from the parents. This stage takes several months, as the toddler learns to explore the surrounding environment while leaving the parents side for a brief time only to return and see the parent still there. This encourages the child to explore even further out and internalize the idea of object constancy. My parents are still there and I am a separate self. The freedom to explore and learn is a hallmark of this stage, yet the parents need to create safe boundaries since the toddler has no understanding of impending danger. Other milestones at this stage are refining motor skills, potty training and other mind body accomplishments. Any premature coaching or forcing of a developmental task can lead to conflict and the toddler expressing their adamant "NO!" If this process is continually overridden by the parent the toddler will feel invaded and controlled.

You can imagine any experiences of repression or humiliation during the toddler phase can lead to a pattern of withholding. The parent's dominance usually wins leading to the suppression of the toddler's agency. Remember, these patterns start off as natural responses to the environment around us. When a significant trauma happens or perpetuates, we find ways to recognize it as a pattern and that in turn creates a habitual response from our energy. In this case, when a child starts to express its individuation and individuality it is met by continuous resistance from the parents or caregivers.

At this stage the toddler becomes confused between being merged with the parent or individuated. The toddler thrives for a separate self yet is unaware of boundaries, space, or any dangers. The family field is the energy container that provides safety, comfort and love until these stages are achieved.

Early concepts of experiences are forming within the developing mind. Sensorimotor, preoperational, concrete operational, and formal operational are earlier modes of cognitive development theorized by Jean Piajet (1969), a swiss psychologist. Each is stage and age specific and focuses on acquiring certain cognitive skills. It also implies that memories at this stage of development may be clouded by the limitation of our cognitive development. Currently there are more complex models that describe cognitive development throughout one's life cycle. For the purpose of understanding trauma, body armoring and contracted breath, we can use these four in exploring how breath, beliefs and emotions can become trapped in the physical body.

The toddler moves through the expressive stage into the integrative stages where ideas, thoughts and experiences are forming concepts and the third level of the human energy field, the human mind,is mapping new ideas and experiences that become incorporated into the subconscious mind as real memories of events. Here is where trauma memories can become embedded in the field. The child remembers events without the ability to consider any other experience than the self. The toddler doesn't understand the danger of running in front of the bus or that they could die if they make certain mistakes. Rather, when the parent startles them by yelling and grabbing their arm. They interpret the experience as; "the parent is angry with me."

You may have felt invaded by your caregiver, perhaps being forced to eat more or given food instead of being allowed to play. There might have been an early push for potty training, where you learned to hold in obstinately with a firm "No." These experiences become internalized, where you feel invaded and learn to create a protective field around your core, and holding it becomes a way to stay safe. Your creative life pulse may have become buried beneath layers of this internalized "No" as a way to preserve yourself. Externally, you became compliant, merging with your primary caregiver, leading to codependent behaviors.

Parenting can be very challenging, especially for new parents. Learning the developmental stages and your child's communication signals is significant in regulating bonding. In the withholding pattern, the toddler learns to reorient and freeze their life pulse deep inside and down into the earth, giving up their authentic freedom to express themselves.

The life pulse contracts inside and is held in stasis, the person loses the full expansion of the expressive phase of the life pulse. As a result, the authentic need to express one's creativity and ideas is withheld deep inside while the person reorients towards the needs from the environment. The part of the creative expression becomes a shield deep inside while other aspects move toward mirroring others and meeting their needs. The pattern is a double-edged sword. "I feel the pleasure in helping others integrate their projects and succeed while at the same time, I may not express my own creative ideas or projects". I go inside at times and don't know what I want. If I am not orienting towards fulfilling others needs, I feel lost, confused and empty. The gift of integration and helping others solidify and ground their projects is worthy of praise and feeling a sense of accomplishment. And, at times, there can be a secret withholding or resentment for not manifesting one's own idea.

Usually, these individuals have internalized and constructed the plans for manifesting a great dream. Yet, they tend to withhold the idea and do not take the steps for fear that it will be taken from them. Unconsciously the sense of invasion is mapped in the psyche and reinforces the pattern. You can notice both the gifts and the compliant withholding pattern held within the physical body structure and armoring. If you have this pattern, you may find yourself sacrificing your own needs in service of others.

Robbins appreciated the endurance and toughness of the withholding pattern and named the character type solidifier. He focused on their strength, stability, and power to endure situations with resilience. Additionally, they can bring all aspects of creation together and consolidate them. They're great to have on a team when working on projects. I prefer to name this stage the integration phase. The toddler is in the process of integrating a sense of self, an internalized sense of, "I am separate from my parents." The rapprochement phase is one of separation and individuation. It is the phase of integration of the outer and inner world.

People exhibiting these patterns are considered thoughtful, compassionate and generous in spirit. They are dependable, steadfast and can endure long hours working on a project. They can integrate many parts and are willing to complete difficult tasks. They often channel their deep feelings into positive actions. They are persistent and consistently work towards completing tasks and goals. Their resilience and strength enables them to face challenges with perseverance, grace and compassion.

Expansive Life Pulse in Contraction
Aggressive Pattern

The aggressive pattern approximately forms around 30 months to 48 months and in some cases as late as seven years of age. Oftentimes, the developmental ranges vary and are a map to the territory of a person's life experiences. I have seen patterns emerge later in life due to similar circumstances, caused by war, depression, suppression and trauma. In this developmental stage, the child becomes the parentified parent for the opposite sexed parent. The child is raised up to be the little "prince or princess," oftentimes feeling special.

This situation sets up an unhealthy dynamic with the same sex parent and usually disrupts healthy bonding. There are many different scenarios that can set this pattern into play. One may be a loss of the same sex parent either through death or divorce. The child can be unconsciously used as a replacement for the missing parent. Another scenario, is when partner's are not emotionally and relationally attentive, the child can be used as an emotional support. The opposite sex parent may share private information about the other parent with the child causing a sense of loyalty to the opposite sex parent and triangulation with the same sex parent. In these cases the child's nervous system and bonding become mapped with these types of situations.

They usually start to pull the energy up into the upper chest and become ungrounded in the root chakra. You can see an upper body displacement when children are rising above it all, and growing up too fast. The betrayal from the same sex parent sets up an inner struggle between "right vs wrong", "bad vs good". The entanglement and triangulation with parents imprints the fear of being the bad one, like the same sex parent, so the child thinks, "I need to be the good one." These internalized cognitive assumptions become seeded deep within the subconscious and form the personality pattern that continues into adulthood.

In adults, the aggressive pattern is easily identified in individuals who are assertive, often taking charge of situations, and control outcomes. They make decisions quickly and confidently, exhibiting a strong, commanding presence that draws attention and respect. With a highly goal-oriented mindset, they prioritize results over relationships and show fearlessness by taking risks and facing challenges head-on. Their communication style is direct and straightforward, often being blunt or outspoken. They naturally take on leadership roles, demonstrating dominance and influence. While they value independence and self-reliance, they might struggle with being sensitive to the needs and feelings of others, sometimes appearing aggressive or uncaring. Additionally, they may have difficulty trusting others, preferring to rely on themselves to maintain control.

Instead of describing this personality pattern as someone who seeks control, Robbins reframes this structure by focusing on the leadership and inspirational qualities that can arise from an aggressive pattern. He called it the "inspirer" character because these people can motivate and inspire others to accomplish goals that may otherwise go unattended. This focuses more on the positive manifestation of the pattern, which is good leadership, charisma, and an ability to inspire others.

Creative/Achiever Life Pulse in Contraction
Contained Pattern

Around six years of age, the child learns how to follow rules and learns the family values and customs. They attend school, follow directions, and become oriented towards what is expected of them. Their behavior is modified by parents, school, social gatherings and religious organizations. During this phase children learn what is expected of them and act appropriately according to the internalized rules. This socialization can impact the child's authentic experiences and self expression.

For example, children are often expected to behave appropriately after witnessing their parents arguing before walking into grandma's house. They are expected to pretend that what just happened in the car never happened, denying their own experiences and feelings. This type of experience of reorienting from one's inner experience to act appropriately on the outside leads to a sense of perfectionism and orderliness. On the outside they are quite organized and look well put together. Their clothes, cars, and closets all look in perfect order. People admire how calm, well put together, and contained these individuals appear. Oftentimes, imagining they have a perfect life.

For the person with the appropriate and contained pattern, their inside world doesn't match the outer world. They have a strong reason and will component with an internalized superego, constantly governing their appropriate behavior. They feel disconnected from their own authenticity and light within. Their emotions are contained in the physical structure that looks well organized and held by muscular tension. They usually remain calm when others are over-expressive, and appear to be denying the reality of the situation. They are waiting for the outer behavior to become contained and appropriate.

If this is your pattern, you might exhibit a strong sense of rules and have a clear understanding of morality and justice. This sense of morality often guides your decisions and actions. For example, you might stand up for someone being treated unfairly, believing it is your duty to uphold justice. These individuals usually follow a set of principles they consider essential. They may spend time reflecting on ethical dilemmas, trying to determine the best course of action based on their values. Their moral compass directs them in both personal and professional spheres, making them focus on doing what they believe is correct. Sometimes, this leads them to take a stand on important issues, pushing for change in their communities or workplaces.

Robbins saw the potential in this character type, noting that individuals with a contained structure can drive themselves toward healthy achievement. He called this the "achiever" character, highlighting their ability to remain calm and organized during times of stress. When you open up to your authenticity, a new liveliness can emerge within your achievement phase, allowing you to experience pleasure from your soul's longing and gifts. Instead of striving for perfection, you can find joy in your accomplishments.

Nature vs. Nurture on Personality Patterns

In our early years of existence, genetics plays an important role in the development of our personality pattern defense styles. Biologically, you inherit certain traits and tendencies from your parents through your DNA. This influences your personality, such as temperament, and how you process emotions and behavioral patterns. For example, if your parents tended to avoid conflict, you may also develop a similar defense style of avoiding confrontation to maintain peace and harmony in relationships. This genetic predisposition can shape how you approach challenges and interact with others throughout your life.

According to studies, some specific genetic makeup can influence how we respond to stress; some people are naturally resilient, while others struggle. As a result, these traits may influence how you react to life experiences and shape your character over time (Buchanan & Lovallo, 2019). Maternal stress during pregnancy is another factor that may contribute. Suppose a mother has high levels of stress. This may impact the developing baby's young brain and potentially affect their ability to regulate emotions and cope with stress later in life.

While genetics provides the blueprint dictating most of your features, the environment in which you grow up also plays a big part in shaping and molding your character. Environmental factors such as upbringing, cultural background, social interactions, and life experiences are critical in developing personality traits.

Growing up in a nurturing and supportive family can foster self-confidence, empathy, and resilience, while growing up in a neglectful environment may lead to the development of insecurity or defensiveness. Daily interactions with classmates, teachers, and other role models can also shape your character. Good relationships and positive role models, such as having close friends or receiving support from teachers, can help to build your self-worth and develop good moral values. On the other hand, negative experiences such as bullying or rejection may cause the development of different defensive or maladaptive character patterns.

Genetic and environmental interactions can also affect your character style. Studies show that certain environments can activate or deactivate certain genes in your body, affecting your stress response and behavior. These may later lead to the development of psychological conditions, such as post-traumatic stress or major depressive disorders (Soliva-Estruch et al., 2023).

Affects on Behavior and Emotions?

As you recall, our personality develops from a set of defense mechanisms that we formed to deal with our emotional pain, abuse, and neglected needs from childhood. These defenses can present themselves as certain behaviors that dictate how you conduct yourself in your day-to-day activities. For instance, if you have a creative pattern, you will most likely display behaviors that involve withdrawal and seclusion in an attempt to prevent rejection or overwhelming emotions. On the other hand, if you have an expressive personality pattern, you might engage in behaviors designed to seek assurance and closeness in an attempt to address an unfulfilled need for care.

Personality patterns can also impact how we solve problems and make decisions. For example, suppose you are highly organized and methodical but struggle to be flexible and adaptable when facing unexpected challenges. This can be the result of having an achiever personality pattern. On the other hand, if you have a withheld pattern, you might avoid taking risks or making decisive choices due to a subconscious fear of punishment or failure.

Suppose you possess an inspirer and aggressive pattern. In that case, you may have an edge in controlling, dominating, manipulating, or competing with others and need a position of power. However, if you have a withheld pattern, you may put up with mistreatment, behave poorly to avoid conflict, or keep the peace outside at your own expense.

Other affective defensive positions include not being able to feel or express emotions. This is common for the achiever pattern and leads to the inability to respond emotionally in relationships, and you might be labeled cold. If, on the other hand, your personality pattern is nurturer (oral), you will process emotions more deeply, act with passion, and feel the need to express and win the approval of others.

Other emotional struggles may be associated with feelings of guilt or unworthiness. If you have a withholding pattern; this results in being submissive or defensive when facing criticism or rejection. Similarly, if you have an achiever personality pattern, you may be hypersensitive to perceived threats to your autonomy, leading to rigid or perfectionistic behaviors.

With this understanding of character analysis, the next chapter will focus on concepts of breath contractions, and later we will explore the relationship between defense styles, breath contractions, and different traits.

Chapter 7:

Breath Contraction

Breathe. Let go. And remind yourself that this very moment is the only one you know you have for sure. –Oprah Winfrey

The blocks in the free flow of the life pulse lead us here to explore breath contraction. In this chapter, we will explore how numerous breathwork pioneers developed the theories around trauma and contracted breath. Breath contractions are characterized by restricted diaphragmatic movement and shallow chest breathing, whereas deep, relaxed breathing fully engages the diaphragm and lung capacity. The first type of breathing can be a habitual pattern if you have experienced prolonged stress, trauma, or anxiety. When the body experiences stress, it instinctively shifts into fight-or-flight mode, activating the sympathetic nervous system, resulting in a faster heart rate, shallow breaths, and tension around the muscles. Over time, continuous exposure to stress will lead to chronic breath contraction, making it difficult to achieve deep, full breaths without conscious effort.

In the previous chapter we discussed what occurs at different stages of development when the life pulse is impacted. Your reactive patterns reflect the contracted state that occurs when you are faced with similar situations and energetic memories from early childhood.

Exploring how your breath moves through the phases of expansion-stasis, contraction-stasis, will give you insight into how your breath flows freely or is contracted. We will explore the five personality patterns of leaving, collapsing, merging, aggressive and contained and where the breath is held within the body. Understanding your pattern will help you explore new breathwork techniques to free the flow of life force and energy in your body while releasing unhealthy patterns.

Concepts of Breath Contraction

A breath contraction is a constrained or shallow breathing pattern often resulting from tension, stress, or emotional blockages. Let's recall Wilhelm Reich's theory on the impact of emotional repression on restricted breathing, chronic muscular tension., and body armoring. His body psychotherapy theories laid the groundwork for psychologists and breathwork pioneers to evolve the field to where it is popular today. In the 1050's, Reich was called a heretic, jailed, and criticized for his forward thinking on energy and consciousness or physical, psychological, relational, and spiritual health.

With the development of bioenergetics, Alexander Lowen, a protege of Reich's, continued to evolve the theories of the correlation between emotional states and physical armoring. He preferred his clients to stand whereas Reich had his patients lie down. Lowen further developed Bio-energetic techniques to release the flow of life force in the body. He pointed out that breath contraction is part of a broader holding pattern, a defense mechanism that traps energy and emotional expression within your body. We will soon look into this in detail.

Later, Barbara Brennan expanded this concept in her field of energy healing. She expressed how restricted breathing disrupts energy flow through the human energy consciousness field, (HECF) including the flow of energy through the chakras. She combined her knowledge of physics and Core Energetics with the emerging field of energy healing. Brennan developed several healing techniques to free trauma, release the emotions and faulty assumptions, and restore coherency on four dimensions of the human energy consciousness system (HECS). The groundbreaking work, along with integration of several disciplines, has inspired many other scientists, psychologists, and change makers in several fields of study. Her work highlighted the importance of restoring natural, full breathing to release energetic blockages and achieve emotional and spiritual balance.

Implications of Breath Contraction

Physically restricted shallow breath can reduce lung capacity and respiratory efficiency. This is due to a lack of full engagement of the diaphragm and other respiratory muscles, resulting in less oxygen delivery to the lower lobes of the lungs, where most of the gaseous exchange takes place. This limits the amount of oxygen that enters the bloodstream, as well as limiting the excretion of carbon dioxide. If not addressed, this could contribute to chronic respiratory impairment, fatigue, and cardiovascular problems.

Breath can also be held tight in the lower abdomen where people hold their fear around being terrorized by war, abuse, or other factors. The person pulls the abdomen in forcing the breath up into the diaphragm and holds it there. This can happen when people feel "Scared Stiff." The abdomen contracts and energy is pulled up along the back of the spine. There are other sayings that indicate how people contract their breath. Have you ever said, "I've been running all day and can barely catch my breath." Next time, notice if you are literally upper chest or thoracic cavity breathing. Or, have you ever felt frightened in a car thinking someone is about to hit your car? Consider how your breath does throughout your day. Take notice of your habitual breathing patterns.

Breath contraction also impacts the flow of energy through the chakras system ultimately contracting or expanding the body. According to Barbara Brennan, breath is the primary vehicle for moving energy through the body. When breathing is shallow or restricted, the energy flow becomes blocked or stagnant, leading to imbalances in the chakra system (Brennan, 1990). For example, if your chest breathing is restricted, this may affect your heart chakra, potentially leading to emotional imbalance—such as feeling disconnected or unloved. Similarly, contracted breath in the lower abdomen can disrupt the root chakra, resulting in a feeling of insecurity. The body's ability to recover and maintain its natural energetic balance might be impaired due to breath tension, which can reduce your well-being.

Your body compensates for restricted or contracted breathing by using secondary muscles in the neck and collarbone rather than relying on the diaphragm. This leads to a slouched posture, rounded shoulders, and the head being pushed forward. Over time, this improper posture strains your neck, back, and shoulder muscles, leading to discomfort and muscle weakness. As these muscles work harder to support your body, they become overworked. Meanwhile the core muscles, including those around your diaphragm, become underused and weak, further contributing to poor posture, mostly felt in the chest, shoulders, and neck, causing you to feel discomfort, stiffness, and pain. The increase in these two vital signs leads to a decrease in oxygen supply to your vital organs. This may cause cardiovascular stress over time.

Contracted breathing causes poor oxygen delivery to your lungs, which puts you at risk of developing cognitive impairment. This can lead to poor concentration, memory problems, mental fog, and impaired decision-making and problem-solving abilities. In addition, prolonged restrictive breathing can weaken your immune system, making it difficult for your body to fight infections and heal effectively.

Moreover, as I mentioned above in the car scenario, habitually contracting the diaphragm muscle inward can lead to development of digestive problems, such as irritable bowel syndrome. This is due to reduced diaphragmatic movements, which massage and activate the digestive organs. Additionally, chronic stress from prolonged breath contractions may exacerbate irritable bowel syndrome or acid reflux.

Patterns of Breath Contraction

Let's explore five different types of breath contraction and how they relate to our personality patterns and defenses. These prolonged contracted states often are hardwired into our deep limbic system as habitual reactive responses, personality patterns, and defense mechanisms. They hijack the original life pulse which ultimately leads you toward creativity, expressiveness, integration, inspiration and achievement. Let's identify these patterns and then discuss how to address them.

Leaving Pattern

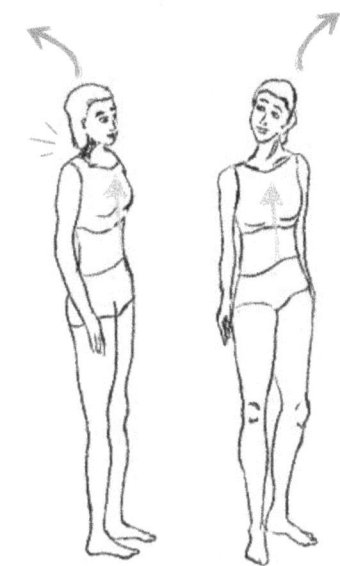

Creative Life Pulse in Contraction
Leaving Pattern

Physically, the leaving pattern may manifest as a weak, fragile body with bad coordination and cohesion as shown in the figure above. The eyes may seem drawn in, the voice tends to be very low, and the body is typically underweight. There is also often one shoulder that is bigger than the other, and tension appears on the back of the neck just below the skull. The energy within the body appears to twist outward and dissipate, giving the impression that the person is ungrounded and has a vacant look in their eyes. In some cases, you may have cold feet and hands more than anything else.

The physical appearance is influenced by their energy structure which is inwardly focused. This pattern describes a tendency for your energy to dissipate or disconnect from your physical body. This can manifest as feeling disoriented, unfocused, or disconnected from the current moment. You may find it difficult to stay grounded, as if you are floating away or not present in your body. This often arises from traumatic experiences, overwhelming emotions, or chronic stress, where your mind and energy leave your body as a form of self-defense from whatever is going on. Over time, this can make it difficult for you to stay present and fully engage with life. Because of your sensitivity, you may also have an energy field that feels porous, absorbing the emotions of others, which can lead to feelings of depletion or emotional overwhelm if you don't establish healthy boundaries.

Breath Position

In the leaving pattern, you will often hold your breath in a shallow, disconnected way. This breath pattern is usually chest-focused and tends to be shallow and fast, reflecting your emotional withdrawal and tendency to detach from the body. Because you are often disconnected from your emotions, breath may feel tense or constricted, especially in your upper chest and throat area. In some cases, the breath may be very minimal, reflecting your difficulty fully engaging with the present moment or with emotional expression.

The constricted breath in leaving personalities can also lead to tension in the shoulders, neck, and diaphragm, as your body may tighten up in an attempt to "hold back" or avoid emotional engagement. The lack of deep, full breaths can create feelings of emotional numbness or disconnection from your body.

Breathing Exercises for the Leaving Pattern

This exercise helps you identify and release the energetic leaving pattern, which we described as a tendency for energy to dissipate from your body, often as a result of trauma or overwhelming stress.

- Begin by finding a firm chair in which you can sit comfortably. Ensure your back is straight and your feet are flat on the floor.

- Next, make a continuous "ah" sound in your normal voice while keeping your eyes on a stopwatch or wristwatch. Aim to sustain the sound for at least 20 seconds.

- Practice this exercise regularly, gradually increasing the time for which you sustain the sound. This will help to mobilize the tight muscles in your chest and allow them to relax.

- You can also perform this exercise by counting aloud in a steady rhythm, which also encourages full expiration and deeper inhalation.

- If you struggle to maintain the sound for 20 seconds, this may indicate that you have some respiratory difficulty. The exercise will help you open up your chest and release deep emotions that you might have suppressed; you may even cry as you release them. Lowen explained that babies have no other way of releasing stress except to cry, which is why it is our principal method of doing so as well. As we're desperate, we cry, but as our urgency fades, we cry even more.

Please do not force yourself to cry or feel the release of these emotions. Allow it to happen naturally. The more you let yourself loose, the more your body will respond, recovering its natural gracefulness and health.

Collapsing Pattern

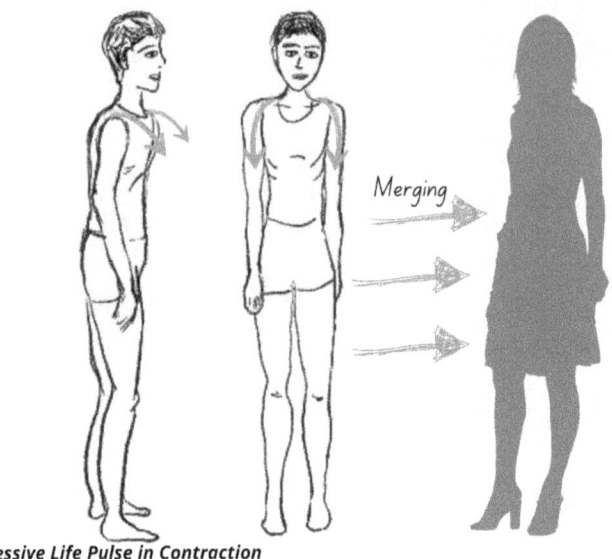

Expressive Life Pulse in Contraction
Collapsing, Merging, Compliant Pattern

The collapsing pattern typically has a soft, rounded, or overly relaxed body type. These individuals often appear plump, soft, or lacking muscle tone, with an emphasis on a rounded, sometimes slouched posture. There's a tendency toward general heaviness or weakness, particularly in the torso and abdomen area.

The posture tends to be collapsed, as if the person is unable or unwilling to stand fully erect or engage in full expression. This collapse may be most apparent in the chest or shoulders, which may round inward, giving the impression of someone who is withdrawn or depressed. Movement tends to be slow, heavy, or listless, and the body may appear reluctant to engage with the world, reflecting a lack of emotional or physical vitality.

The energy field of the Collapsing Pattern tends to be weak, contracted, and directed toward the other. This results in an energy field that feels shrunken or drained.

There is an overwhelming lack of vitality, which may feel like emotional exhaustion, depletion, or apathy. Rather than flowing freely, the energy is often stuck or repressed, causing a feeling of being disconnected from the life pulse. Despite this contraction, when the expressive life pulse begins to break through, it often comes out in explosive bursts of emotional release, which may feel overwhelming or uncontrollable. These bursts tend to be sporadic and uncontained, as the energy that's been blocked for so long tries to escape all at once, leading to emotional breakdowns or moments of intense vulnerability.

Breath Position

The Collapsing Pattern breath is typically shallow, restricted, and focused in the chest, particularly in the upper chest or throat area. Their breathing tends to be difficult or labored, as they have trouble fully expanding the lungs or engaging in deep, full breaths. The breath tends to be erratic, reflecting the internal tension and struggle to release emotional energy. There is a feeling of collapse in their breath pattern, as though they can barely catch their breath, or they may have difficulty maintaining a consistent breath flow.

The restricted breath often leads to a tightening of the diaphragm, causing discomfort in the upper chest and neck, and even leading to digestive issues or chronic fatigue. The collapse of the chest can contribute to feelings of weight or heaviness, as though the person is carrying a physical burden of emotional depression or dissociation. This shallow breathing can also result in a general reliance on external sources, such as food, substances, or people to fill the void they may feel inside. It can also make it difficult for them to fully take in emotional experiences or life energy, contributing to their emotional flatness or lack of expression.

Breathing Exercises for the Collapsing Pattern

The collapsing pattern involves energy withdrawing inward, leading to a sense of physical and emotional drainage. This exercise is designed to help you renew that collapsed energy within you.

- To begin, sit in the same position as in the exercise for the leaving pattern on a sturdy chair with your back straight.

Spend one minute breathing normally to relax.

- Now, start breathing out while making a groaning sound for the entire length of your exhalation. Enjoy the sensation of air being expelled from your body.

- Try to make the same groaning sound during the next inhalation. At first, this might be challenging, but with practice, you will feel the forceful pull of air into your body.

- Make a groaning sound for three full breaths, then split your exhalation into "ugh, ugh" sounds of sobbing. Continue vocalizing during inhalation. If the exhalation is deep, filling your abdomen, it may lead to involuntary crying, which is a natural release of tension.

- If you have been holding onto or have a buildup of anger, crying won't be enough to help fully expand your chest if it is deflated. You will need a much more aggressive approach.

- To release this anger, you can perform the following exercise of hitting a bed from a standing position.

- For stability, bend your knees. Raise your fists above your head and keep your arms close to your ears. Keep your shoulders relaxed and slightly bend your elbows.

- Inhale deeply three times, stretching back with each breath. After your third breath, deliver a forceful punch to the bed while exhaling. Repeat 10–20 times. This frequently leads to a spontaneous release of anger or tears, resulting in a rejuvenated feeling of emotional release.

- Crying during this exercise is a powerful way to release tension and restore emotional balance. It is necessary to break through the contained, tight feelings that may be suppressing your natural breath.

- If you don't feel sad when you start crying, don't worry. This often indicates a detachment from your deeper emotions, which are emerging as your body eases into relaxation.

Withholding Pattern

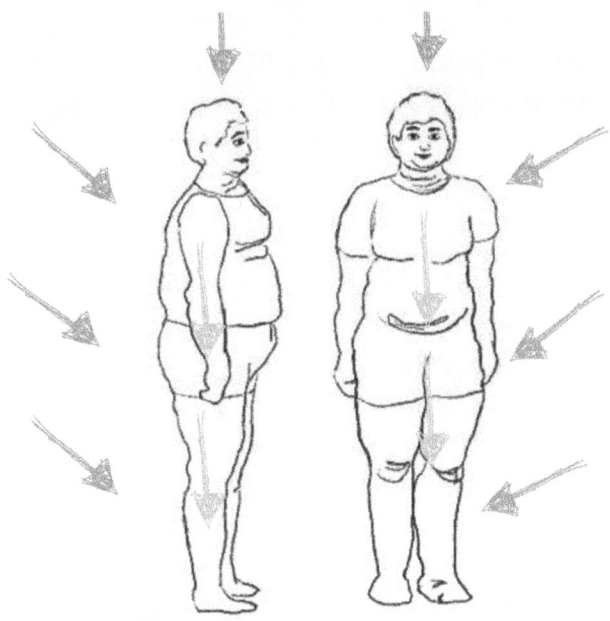

Integrative Life Pulse In Contraction
Withholding , Merging, Compliant Pattern

The withholding pattern, also known as Enduring Type, often presents with a solid, sturdy, or muscular body type. These individuals typically have a dense, heavier build, which reflects their capacity to endure emotional and physical pain. Their frame may appear rigid or tense, with a tendency toward muscular development in the upper body, especially the shoulders, neck, and jaw as a result of holding tension or pushing through difficulty.

A person with this pattern often appears stiff or overly controlled, as though bracing against life's challenges. They might display a stoic, rigid, and compacted posture, often with tight shoulders and a clenched jaw—a physical manifestation of their inner resilience and resistance to vulnerability. Movements may be slow, deliberate, and controlled, reflecting their focus on self-discipline and endurance. However, these individuals also tend to hold themselves back from full expression, often keeping their body in a contracted state to manage their internal experience.

The energy field of the withholding pattern is often contracted, but with a deep, enduring force that seeks to integrate and process difficult emotions. Their energy tends to be stagnant or blocked, particularly in the solar plexus and heart areas, as they hold onto emotional pain, suffering, or unresolved grief. While their energy is strong and resilient, it can become stuck in these areas due to their tendency to endure suffering rather than express or release it.

The integrative life pulse is also in contraction here, meaning the person often struggles to fully engage with the natural flow of life energy. They may feel as though they are constantly pushing through life, enduring hardship, and never fully releasing or healing their pain. Their energy is heavy, dense, and resistant, often lacking the free-flowing, vital energy that comes with emotional release and integration. Instead, it feels suppressed or trapped, as they carry their burdens internally, often neglecting their emotional needs in favor of self-sacrifice or resilience.

Breath Position

The breath in the withholding pattern is typically shallow and tends to be held high in the chest, often accompanied by a tightening of the diaphragm. The person may hold their breath as a response to emotional tension, reflecting their tendency to suppress or endure discomfort without fully acknowledging it. Their breathing may feel labored or constrained, particularly when they are trying to manage feelings of helplessness or pain. The breath is typically shallow and restricted, staying in the upper chest and solar plexus area, and it can often become faster or more erratic during moments of stress or emotional overload.

The high chest and throat-based breathing is a clear sign of emotional constriction. There is often a holding of the breath during moments of perceived stress or pain, as the individual attempts to manage or suppress their emotional responses. This tightness can contribute to neck, shoulder, and chest tension, as the person physically braces against emotional overwhelm. The breath can sometimes become more erratic when they are under emotional strain, but it rarely descends into the abdomen, as there is a conscious or unconscious effort to avoid deeper emotional engagement.

The tight chest, clenched jaw, and tense shoulders are common physical manifestations of their breath pattern. Over time, this shallow breathing can lead to chronic tension in the upper body, particularly in the neck, shoulders, and diaphragm. There can also be a feeling of tightness in the stomach or solar plexus, as they may be holding onto feelings of unresolved anger, fear, or sadness. The lack of deep, relaxing breath can also make it difficult for them to process and release stored emotional energy, leading to physical discomfort or dis-ease in the body.

Breathing Exercises for the Withholding Pattern

The purpose of this exercise is to assist you in releasing energy that is stored deep within your body. Participating in this exercise will help you open up the flow of your life pulse and reconnect with your natural energy.

- Start by getting into a comfortable position, whether it's on a cushion, a mat, or your bed. Once you're settled, focus on feeling your natural breathing pattern and observe your life pulse rhythm for the first few minutes. Pay attention to any areas in your body where you feel blocked or where energy feels withheld.

- Next, breathe consciously, ensuring air expands from your abdomen, into your diaphragm then into your upper chest. Allow yourself to be aware of any feelings or thoughts that arise regarding what you may be withholding. Is it your passion or creative gifts? Are you holding back any of your emotions or thoughts? Spend a minute contemplating these questions without judgment.

- Next, start fluttering, kicking your feet back and forth while maintaining awareness of your breath. Later, include your arms, moving them along with your legs. Do this for five minutes, allowing yourself to engage in a temper tantrum kind of motion. This may feel difficult at first, but as you continue, try to release any tension or pent-up emotions that may be stored in your body. Remember that the energy you're withholding is your life pulse trying to move through you.

- Releasing this stored energy opens pathways for self-expression and frees you from internal blocks. Allow the energy to flow freely and notice how this affects your breath and emotional state.

This involves consciously or unconsciously restraining or inhibiting your emotions, thoughts, or energetic flow. This may stem from fear, self-doubt, or a need to maintain control. With this pattern, you might notice tension in your chest, shallow breathing, or a rigid posture. You may feel as if you're holding your breath or are unable to express yourself fully. This creates blockages that prevent the free flow of life force throughout your body. This can eventually result in chronic stress, anxiety, and a feeling of immobility.

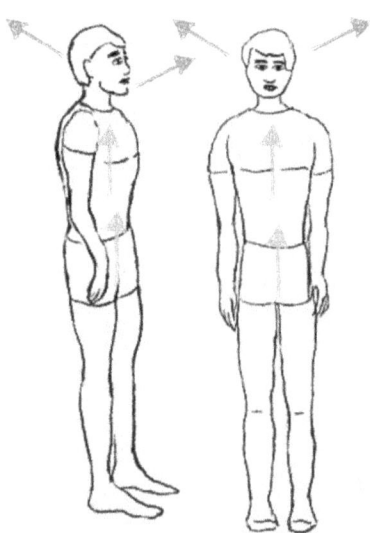

Expansive Life pulse in Contraction
Aggressive or Controlling Pattern

Aggressive Pattern

The Aggressive Pattern often has a muscular, forceful, and physically imposing body type. This individual's body typically reflects strength and power, with a broad chest and well-defined muscles. They may appear rigid, tense, or a bit overbearing, especially in their posture, as though always ready for action or in a state of aggression.

The aggressive pattern carries a dominant posture that is upright or even forward-leaning, conveying a sense of confidence and assertiveness. They tend to move with purpose, their body language often sharp or intense, reflecting a heightened level of energy or agitation. There can be a sense of physical control or tightness, particularly around the jaw, neck, and shoulders, which reflects an internal tension or anger that is ready to be released at any moment. Their movements may appear quick or jerky, often betraying an underlying sense of impatience or aggression.

The energy field of the aggressive type is often explosive, overstimulated, and charged with intense, aggressive energy. When the excitation life pulse is in contraction, their energy becomes blocked, yet still forceful and intense. They are highly reactive and may struggle with the impulse to release energy too quickly or explosively, leading to energy stagnation or buildup.

The excitation life pulse is agitated in this type, meaning they often experience a high level of tension or frustration, particularly in the face of restrictions or challenges. The energy field can feel charged with unresolved aggression, and the individual may find themselves becoming overstimulated, frustrated, or prone to outbursts when they feel confined or unable to release their intense emotions.

The energy flow tends to be blocked or repressed in certain areas, such as the throat, solar plexus, and neck, which can create a sense of physical pressure or tightness. This contraction creates an internal buildup of energy, which is often released abruptly or explosively. The individual may be able to exert force or aggressive will at any given moment, but the natural flow of energy is often interrupted, creating a cycle of intensity and release.

Breath Position

The breath for the aggressive pattern is typically shallow, quick, and often held in the upper chest or throat. This individual's breath is erratic, as they constantly hover between hyper-arousal and aggressive tension. The breath may feel short and labored, as if they are struggling to control or contain their powerful emotions.

Their chest and throat are the main areas where the breath is focused, reflecting the intense energy that is pent up in these regions. As they hold back or try to suppress their impulses, the upper chest can feel particularly tight or tense, as though their breath is stuck or caught in their chest. There is often a quickening of the breath, reflecting the overstimulation of their energy systems. During moments of emotional distress or frustration, their breath may become rapid, superficial, or even suspended, indicating their struggle to manage their inner turbulence.

This restricted or fast-paced breath creates a physical tension in the upper chest, throat, and neck, often leading to tightness or pain in these areas. They might feel like they cannot catch their breath fully, reflecting their internal battle with the need for release versus the pressure to control their aggressive impulses. In some cases, the jaw may tighten or clench, and their posture may become even more rigid and forward-leaning, creating a sense of impending action or explosion.

This pattern is characterized by a sudden, intense release of energy that has been pent up or suppressed. This can come out as a powerful outburst when you've been holding back strong emotions such as anger, frustration, or passion, and can come out as a powerful outburst. This may manifest as a rapid exhalation, aggressive gestures, or even a loud voice. You might also experience a surge of anger, rage, or intense passion that feels uncontrollable in the moment. Further, this pattern represents a break in the usual flow of energy where, instead of a steady release, there is a powerful surge that is overwhelming for you and those around you.

Breathing Exercises for the Aggressive Pattern

In this exercise, we will stretch the abdominal and back muscles to restore full, easy breathing.

- Start by sitting on a chair and breathing in and out. Then, lean back, raise your arms, and take several deep breaths. Do you notice how difficult it is to breathe deeply in this position?

- To overcome this, use a bioenergetic stool or foam roller to expand your collapsed abdomen. Lie over a bioenergetic stool with your feet on the ground and your arms reaching back to a chair. This position stretches your back muscles, which must relax to allow full, effortless breathing. Try not to stiffen against any discomfort you may feel. As you relax into the position, your breathing should become deeper and fuller.

- Alternatively, if you don't have a bioenergetic stool, you can use an old wooden kitchen stool and a large foam roller or the arm of your couch.

- Remember, it's important not to push or force the exercise. If you are experiencing pain or are very uncomfortable, you should not hesitate to stop.

- This exercise is particularly helpful for those who find it difficult to breathe deeply due to a collapsed posture or upper body displacement. Straightening out the abdomen and relaxing the back muscles opens up your respiratory pathway for fuller breathing.

Practicing these exercises will help you reconnect with your breath, release deeply held tensions, and restore balance to your life.

Contained Pattern

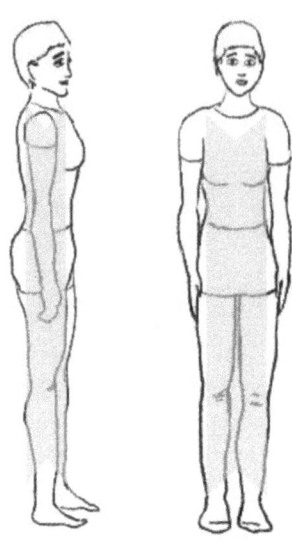

Creative-Achieving Life pulse in Contraction
Contained or Rigid Pattern

Under the contained pattern Your energy will be pulled upward in your body, with diaphragmatic holding in your upper chest and your shoulders pulled up in a defensive position. Your hips may be tilted back, closing off your connection to feeling safe and grounded. This gives you an imposing body that conceals inner fears or insecurities and radiates strength and power.

This pattern is characterized by the absence of movement in your breath, where breathing becomes shallow, minimal, or almost nonexistent. This occurs in response to fear, trauma, or shock, where your body instinctively freezes as a form of protection. You might notice that your breath becomes so shallow that it's barely noticeable, and your body might feel tense or rigid. This stillness can be associated with feelings of numbness and dissociation. This causes a blockage in your natural flow of life force, leading to increased feelings of distress if not addressed.

The contained pattern typically has a stiff, rigid, or immovable body type. This type's physical form is often muscular but dense, with a tendency toward physical heaviness or tightness. There is a broadness to their body, especially in the torso, chest, and neck, which may appear overdeveloped in certain areas due to chronic muscular tension.

The contained pattern typically presents with an upright, unyielding posture, often standing or sitting as though they are braced for something. Their movements are controlled, deliberate, and linear, often appearing mechanical or overly structured. They may seem to be locked in place, reflecting their tendency to hold on tightly to control, structure, or a particular belief system. The muscles are often tense in the neck, jaw, and shoulders, contributing to their unmoving or fixed nature. When they move, it's often with great effort, and they can appear slow or deliberate, which emphasizes their resistance to change or flexibility.

The energy field of the contained pattern is tight, constricted, and often feels stagnant or blocked. Their manifest life pulse, which relates to the individual's ability to express their physical presence and engage with reality, is in contraction. This means their natural flow of energy is restricted and bottled up, often resulting in a sense of internal pressure or frustration. The individual may experience a constant tension between their need to hold onto control and the natural flow of energy that is trying to move through them.

The energy flow is often rigid, following set patterns or rules, reflecting their need for control and structure. In moments of emotional tension, the energy is not easily released; instead, it gets stuck in certain areas, often in the upper body (especially the chest and shoulders). This can lead to feelings of emotional numbness, disconnection, or inflexibility, as the person may be unable to relax or let go of their tightly held beliefs or emotions.

The energy pulse is stuck in their physical expression, preventing the free movement of energy throughout their body. This leads to a lack of spontaneity or fluidity, making their energy feel inhibited or even stifled.

Breath Position

The breath for the contained pattern tends to be shallow and restricted, focused in the upper chest or throat area. Their breathing is typically tight, as though they are holding or controlling their breath, which mirrors their tight grip on life. This shallow breath prevents them from engaging with their full capacity for energy, leaving them feeling disconnected from the natural flow of life.

The breath is often labored or hesitant, as though there's an internal struggle between wanting to release tension and the instinct to maintain control. The diaphragm is not fully engaged, and the abdomen may remain stiff or tight. The breath may even feel like it's trapped in the throat, preventing the person from taking in a full, deep breath. As they attempt to breathe, it may feel as though they are holding back, reflecting their struggle to relinquish control and surrender to the flow of life or emotions.

The tightness in the neck, jaw, and chest is often accompanied by a stiffening or freezing in the rest of the body. Muscle tension in these areas, particularly in the shoulders and upper back, can create a sense of physical rigidity that mimics their emotional blockages. This pattern can lead to chronic discomfort or stiffness, and may even result in physical symptoms like headaches, shoulder pain, or chronic fatigue, as the person holds onto their energy and emotions without letting them release.

Breathing Exercises for the Contained Pattern

In this exercise, movement is important. Learning to relax and let go. Choose two or three different pieces of music to move to. Choose both slow and fast rhythm pieces, you can choose classic, jazz, hip-hop or rock.

- Allow yourself to stand and relax your body while listening to the music. What part of your body moves first, second, etc. Notice your breath. How is your breath restricted?

- Focus on inhaling into a movement and exhaling in the next movement. Notice any armoring or where you feel self-conscious and restrict movement. Bring your attention and focus to your breath and movement.

Breathing Through Trauma

In this section, we are going to focus on breathing through trauma and contractions following techniques inspired by Barbara Brennan's books, specifically *Hands of Light, Light Emerging,* and *Core Light Healing*.

In the previous chapters, we have examined some of Barbara Brennan's work and seen that she also focused on characterology and the flow of energy through our bodies. In her book *Hands of Light: A Guide to Healing Through the Human Energy Field,* she described how traumatic experiences trigger defensive reactions in both our physical body and the human biofield, which is the energetic field within and around us (Brennan, 1990). These defensive reactions often lead to prolonged physical and energetic contractions that can disrupt the natural flow of energy in our bodies.

In *Core Light Healing,* Brennan further explored how trauma affects the human energy consciousness system (HECS), which is the field of energy that is within us and surrounds our bodies. She noted that when trauma occurs, our life force energy contracts or curls in on itself as a form of self-protection (Brennan, 2017). This defensive reaction creates an energetic time capsule; if you recall, in Chapter 5 we described time capsules as pockets of trapped energy within the body's energy field that hold unresolved negative emotions. Over time, these capsules can accumulate and become layered with repeated experiences of trauma, leading to feelings of self-doubt, shame, and worthlessness.

These exercises will focus on releasing all the trauma you have been holding in; they will also help to work through breath contractions.

To participate in this exercise, find a comfortable place to lie down. You can control the environment to your liking by playing calming music, dimming the lights, or whatever brings relaxation.

These exercises focus on using your breath to uncover and release long-held trauma.

As you lie down, take deep, natural breaths until you get into curiosity and observation mode. This approach will enable you to act like a witness to your emotions, memories, and physical sensations. As you breathe into any emotions that arise, you may experience sadness, anger, guilt, or shame. Do not block these emotions; let them flow without passing any judgment.

Next, breathe out the negative emotions as you exhale. Concentrating on the "ahh" breath as you exhale helps you release trapped energy. As you continue to breathe, think back on instances that caused you to experience similar feelings in the past. This may lead to you discovering patterns that define your memories and long-held emotions. Give yourself some time to breathe through each stage of reflection and let go of any residual feelings. With the residual energy out, you can now breathe in different types of energy qualities and observe the results. Below are exercises that show you how to breathe in different qualities of energy and release negative traits from various parts of the body.

Breathe In Trust, Breathe Out Mistrust

While lying down, maintain a comfortable position and focus on breathing into the lower abdomen. As you inhale, imagine breathing in a sense of trust, renewing trust in yourself, others, and the world. Feel your breath expand from the lower abdomen to the pelvic floor.

Next, exhale and visualize feelings of mistrust or insecurity leaving your body. Feel the sense of trust flow through your body as you repeat this breathing cycle.

Breathe In Love, Breathe Out Hurt or Pain

As you breathe, focus your attention on your heartbeat. During inhalation, imagine filling your chest with air that is full of love. Let this sensation spread throughout your heart as you breathe in more air.

When it's time to exhale, attach any hurt or pain you may be holding onto to the air you will breathe out. As you release these feelings, imagine your breath clearing out any blockages or emotional pain stored in your heart.

Breathe In Self-Love and Self-Acceptance
Breathe Out Self-Judgment

Here, you will focus on bringing in self-love and acceptance while inhaling. Embrace and feel self-love and acceptance flowing throughout your body as it washes out any doubts or fears. While breathing out, let the air you exhale expel any self-judgment or self-criticism. Repeating this exercise will replace the negativity within with compassion for yourself.

Breathe In Self-Respect
Breathe Out Disrespect

You will focus your breath on your lower abdomen once again to breathe in self-respect. Take a deep breath and imagine breathing in self-respect, strengthening the light and strength within you. Next, start breathing out while releasing any feelings of disrespect or self-deprecation. You can concentrate on feeling your diaphragm and abdomen softening as you release tension or holding patterns in this area.

We have now looked into exercises that can help you with breath contraction and free you from any childhood-related trauma. From here, it is only suitable that we explore how to care for our health and wellness. In our next chapter, we will focus on maintaining our physical and mental health to enjoy life's benefits to the fullest.

Chapter 8:

Health and Wellness

He who has health, has hope; and he who has hope, has everything. –Thomas Carlyle

We live in a fast-paced world where human needs and wants are changing every day. We may be occupied with pursuing our careers and striving for greatness, and when we choose to relax, most of us tend to spend our time on our gadgets. While pursuing our goals and keeping up with the digital world is commendable, our hectic schedules often lead us to neglect our health.

Most people think of health as a lack of disease, but there is more to it than that. According to the World Health Organization, health can be defined as a state of complete physical, mental, and social well-being, not merely the absence of disease or infirmity (Schramme, 2023).

Fitness and wellness are something to take seriously on a physical, emotional, and spiritual level. If you neglect your health, your body will eventually force you to prioritize it through diseases or mental breakdowns.

This chapter explores the importance of physical, emotional, and spiritual health and how you can nourish each one. We will also look at some practical techniques and workouts to help you achieve a balanced and fulfilling life that allows the free flow of energy within your body, which will eventually have an impact on your surrounding world.

Physical Health

We use physical health as a parameter to assess the condition of our bodies. To be physically fit means maintaining a healthy weight, engaging in regular exercise, and getting enough rest. It also involves nourishing our bodies with nutritious foods and staying hydrated to support overall well-being. In this section, we will explore the importance of breathwork in physical health and how taking care of your body can contribute to the free flow of life, which will impact your mental and emotional well-being as well.

Being physically healthy is having all the different parts of your being aligned to the purpose that you are working towards. In order to fully express the blessings that are within you, you need to have energy flowing through your body and mind freely. This state brings a lot of health benefits, and we are going to look at some of them now.

Cardiovascular exercise reduces hypertension and stroke risk. Research indicates this type of exercise strengthens the heart, lowers blood pressure and boosts metabolism. It also lowers risk of diabetes by lowering insulin levels. In addition to this, it also enhances metabolism which in turn helps to manage your weight. Regular exercise does this by burning calories during workout sessions. Frequent exercise further lowers the risk of metabolic diseases, such as diabetes, by improving insulin sensitivity and regulating the amount of sugar in the blood.

Exercise will also boost blood circulation and detoxify the body through sweat, promoting clearer, healthier skin. Exercises help to slow down aging by producing collagen, which helps to maintain skin elasticity and reduce wrinkles. It also helps reduce inflammation and acne, leading to a more radiant complexion, to match the bright light that shines from your core.

Consistent workouts support improved posture, flexibility, and coordination, thereby preventing energy blockages. This ensures that the life pulse moves smoothly to support your efforts. Endorphins, sometimes referred to as the feel-good hormones, are released which will impact your emotions and mood. When you exercise, these contribute to decreased stress, ultimately increasing your energy levels, and improving your psychological health.

Breath and Immunity

Your body has a physical defense system—the immune system—and we can use breath to fortify and strengthen it. This system is responsible for fighting off harmful pathogens and keeping you healthy. But wait, did you know that there is a link between your breath and your immune system?

You can trace this link back to your body's physiological response to stress. Do you recall the fight-or-flight response we talked about in earlier chapters? Stress triggers an increase in stress hormones such as cortisol, which can weaken your immune system, leaving you vulnerable to illness. On the other hand, regular breathwork exercises, such as pranayama or diaphragmatic breathing, can help increase the production of anti-inflammatory proteins while reducing stress hormones such as cortisol. This can eventually improve your immune system and help you stay healthy. Moreover, breathwork practices can increase oxygenation throughout your body, improving the efficiency of immune cells such as lymphocytes and natural killer cells, which are critical in defending the body against germs.

The connection between breath and immunity doesn't stop with the above. Nasal breathing and controlling your minute volume (also known as MV), which is the amount of air you breathe per minute, can help keep a balance of important gases such as oxygen, carbon dioxide, and nitric oxide in your airways and bloodstream. Research indicates that by reducing your minute volume through nasal breathing, you can enhance the levels of nitric oxide and carbon dioxide, both of which act as potent vasodilators and bronchodilators. This relaxation of your blood vessels and airways ensures the efficient delivery of oxygen-rich blood throughout your body. Moreover, the increased presence of carbon dioxide helps regulate oxygen delivery from hemoglobin to your cells, supporting optimal cellular function (White, 2024). Further, nitric oxide plays a significant role in soothing the nasal and lung mucosa, making it easier for your body to defend itself against harmful germs.

Another study suggests that breathing-induced changes in the pH levels of your airway surfaces can contribute to the destruction of harmful bacteria. This finding points to new therapeutic strategies for improving pulmonary health, especially by optimizing breath patterns to support natural bacterial defense mechanisms (McCarty, 2021).

Taking care of your physical body is one of the most important ways to promote a free flow of the life pulse. Our bodies act as vessels for the creative pulse, allowing it to flow through. Imagine your body as a water pipe, with water serving as the creative pulse. Unmaintained water pipes increase the likelihood of dirty water flowing through your tap due to clogs, and a blockage may result in minimal or no water flow. Similarly, neglecting your physical health can block or disrupt your life pulse, leading to the various complications we've discussed in previous chapters. Neglecting your body due to a busy life often results in blockages or disruptions in the life pulse, leading to energetic stagnation. As a result, you may experience muscle tension, poor posture, or chronic physical pain.

Regular exercise, proper nutrition, and sufficient rest are some of the key ways to promote the free flow of the life pulse. Physical activity facilitates the release of stored, pent-up energy in the body, thereby clearing blocked channels. Exercise stimulates an increase in blood flow throughout the body, including to the brain; this boosts cognitive function and mental clarity. It also helps the life pulse expand and contract without difficulty, preventing it from becoming stuck in a state of stasis or contraction.

Good nutritional balance provides the essential building blocks and energy our bodies need. The nutrients found in our diet help maintain our cells, organs, muscles, and bones. You can think of nutrients as a way to preserve and repair a water pipe for the free flow of water. Similarly, if you throw food particles from your sink down the drain, those particles will likely clog or block the pipes that carry used water. Our bodies work the same way: Poor nutrition starves the body of essential nutrients, which increases the risk of disease and poor function.

Another important way of maintaining excellent health is through hydration, which helps regulate body temperature, transport nutrients and oxygen to cells, and remove waste products from the body.

It is also important to get enough sleep to maintain the body's excellent health. The body requires rest to recover from the day's activities. During this rest, the body rebuilds its tissues and muscles and produces the hormones necessary for cell growth and appetite. Similar to breathing, sleep is also important for immune function. Research shows that well-rested people have better immunity against diseases.; conversely, other studies have linked sleep deprivation to obesity, cardiovascular disease, and diabetes (Garbarino et al., 2021). Moreover, sufficient amounts of sleep are good for efficient thinking, learning, and emotional control. These advantages demonstrate how rest can support life's flow. When we are well rested, our life pulse is more open and free to be creative, think more clearly, and be emotionally stronger.

In addition, studies show that sufficient sleep enhances brain plasticity, which helps the brain develop the new connections and ideas that are critical in problem-solving and innovation. A lack of sleep, on the other hand, can also affect your mental state, leading to rigid and emotionally unstable thinking that can impede the flow of your life pulse. Therefore, by choosing rest, we create the optimal conditions for our lives to flourish, leading to increased involvement and creativity in our interactions with our surroundings.

Physical Exercises to Improve Health

Now that we've explored the benefits of exercise, if you don't currently work out, you may be wondering how you can start, what type of exercises are most effective, and how long you should work out to keep your physical vessel in the best shape for the life pulse to flow.

To get started, you need to know that different exercise programs are tailored according to different needs, be it for fitness, weight loss, or muscle gain. For fitness purposes, the World Health Organization (2020), recommends engaging in at least

150 minutes of moderate-intensity aerobic physical activity throughout the week, or 75 minutes of vigorous-intensity aerobic physical activity. You can break this down into smaller segments, such as exercising for 30 minutes daily, five days a week. If this seems excessive, you can begin with 10–15 minutes of daily exercise, gradually increasing the duration and intensity as you become accustomed to it. The key is to be consistent and choose a schedule that is not burdensome. While exercising, listen to your body and consult your doctor if you have medical conditions to determine which type of exercise is best for you.

It is undeniable that breathing plays a huge role in physical performance. How you breathe during exercise can significantly influence your stamina, strength, and overall performance. At rest, the normal respiratory rate falls between 12 and 20 breaths per minute. However, during exercise, this rate can increase up to 40–60 breaths per minute, depending on the intensity of your workout. This change in respiratory rate allows for increased oxygen intake, which fuels your muscles, as well as the removal of carbon dioxide, which helps maintain balance within your body as oxygen demands rise.

Practicing safe breathing techniques also helps you avoid injury, stay safe, and recover faster post-workout. Another benefit of correct breathing during exercise is its ability to improve posture. This is because some of the muscles involved in breathing are key muscles that help you sit and stand upright, promoting proper alignment and reducing strain on your back and neck.

Below, we'll explore effective breathing methods that can boost your physical performance and support your overall well-being. Let us look at some of the main types of exercise you might want to add to your life.

Strength Training

Firstly, we have strength training, which focuses on building muscle strength and endurance. These exercises include activities such as resistance band exercises and bodyweight movements like squats, lunges, push-ups, and weightlifting. The main aim of this category of exercise is to improve muscle tone and bone density. These exercises also help improve the metabolic rate, resulting in better weight management and energy balance. Targeting all important muscle groups in a well-rounded routine helps prevent injuries, correct posture, and support joint health.

In strength training, your breath can support your core muscles and help prevent any form of injury. Breathing out during the effort phase of an exercise and breathing in during the relaxation phase is a beneficial technique for strength training. This technique, known as the Valsalva maneuver, entails taking a deep breath, holding it, and contracting your core muscles while applying pressure, such as during weightlifting. This method supports your spine and core muscles when performing strenuous workouts like deadlifts or squats by creating intra-abdominal pressure. Let's look into how to apply breath control to various exercises:

Squats

If you are doing squats, start by standing tall with your feet shoulder-width apart, taking a deep breath to fill your lungs, and holding your breath as you begin to lower yourself into the squatting position. Slowly exhale through your mouth as you push yourself back up to the starting position. Breathe normally before you repeat the cycle.

Deadlifts

If your focus is on deadlifts, breathing control can help stabilize your spine, helping you to balance with good posture, prevent injury, and increase your energy and strength. Start by placing your feet hip-width apart with your toes under the barbell. Before you bend to grip the bar, take a deep breath in and contract your muscles. Hold this breath as you lift the barbell off the ground. As you complete the lift, keep holding the breath to ensure stability. Once you're standing fully upright with the weight, exhale slowly. While standing, inhale again before lowering the weight, then exhale as you lower the bar. To ensure you maximize your deadlift exercises, repeat these steps depending on the target reps you have set.

Bench Press

Although this is a popular workout in the gym, many people struggle to fully utilize it due to poor breathing habits during their workouts. Coordinating your breath with a bench press can help you maximize your pressing power. To begin, lie on the bench with your eyes aligned under the barbell. As you unrack the bar, take a deep breath in. This breath will help create tension in your upper body. Hold your breath while lowering the bar toward your chest to maintain stability and control. This will help you maintain chest and core stability. As you press the bar back up, start to exhale slowly and steadily. This controlled exhale will help you maintain tension while avoiding the lightheadedness caused by holding your breath for too long. Before starting the next rep, breathe in until you've fully extended your arms. This breathing pattern will give your bench press a consistent rhythm and help you maintain proper form throughout your set.

If you have cardiovascular challenges, you should exercise caution when holding your breath because it raises blood pressure. It is always advisable to contact a healthcare practitioner before beginning any new fitness plan, especially if you have any underlying health issues.

Flexibility and Cardiovascular Exercises

Yoga and Pilates are examples of flexibility exercises. These exercises focus on stretching muscles and improving range of motion, which is important for maintaining joint motion and reducing muscle stiffness. They also improve blood circulation, prevent muscle imbalances, and contribute to better coordination and balance.

As we age, exercises help us improve stability and prevent falls. They also help enhance proprioception, which is our body's ability to sense movement and position. Examples of balance exercises include standing on one leg, heel-to-toe walking, and tai chi. These exercises are useful if you want to maintain independence and quality of life as you age.

Then there are exercises like walking, running, swimming,

and cycling which are examples of aerobic exercise, which are important for maintaining cardiovascular health. These activities improve heart and lung function, increase stamina, and enhance tissue oxygen delivery. Participating in moderate to vigorous aerobic activity regularly can lower the risk of heart disease, hypertension, and diabetes.

If you are not strength training or if your focus is on cardio workouts, having your breath in synchronization with your movement is an efficient way to optimize your physical performance. When running, you can use the 2:2 pattern, a common rhythmic breathing pattern. This simple method requires you to inhale every two steps and exhale after the next two steps. This technique ensures a steady flow of oxygen to your muscles and prevents early fatigue. Other exercises where you can apply rhythmic breathing include the following:

Cycling

Cycling is one of the best cardiovascular exercises for improving circulation and endurance. While cycling, synchronize your breathing with your pedal strokes: Inhale every four pedal strokes and exhale every four pedal strokes. This 4:4 pattern can help you sustain a steady rhythm and pace during long cycling distances. If you choose to cycle intensely, you might switch to a 3:3 or even a 2:2 pattern, adjusting based on your exertion level.

Swimming

You can apply the same principle when swimming—simply inhale every three strokes to ensure consistent oxygen intake while maintaining your swimming rhythm.

Jump rope

For jump rope exercises, try breathing in for four jumps and out for four jumps. This 4:4 pattern can help you maintain your stamina and prevent you from getting winded too quickly. As you become more proficient, you can adjust to a 3:3 or 2:2 pattern for more intense sessions.

Diaphragmatic Breathing

Although diaphragmatic breathing can be used as a standalone exercise, it can also be applied during physical activity. This deep breathing technique, which we explored in Chapter 4, helps improve oxygen intake, increases respiratory efficiency, aids in supplying the muscles with more oxygen and nutrition, and assists in overcoming fatigue while you work out. You can apply diaphragmatic breathing during long-distance runs, cycling, or yoga.

Breathing Techniques for Recovery

After a workout session, it's important to allow your body to recover, and one of the ways to do this is to breathe. During your post-workout stretching session, you can try employing the 4–7–8 breathing technique. With each stretch, whether it's a hamstring stretch or a shoulder stretch, take a deep breath in for four seconds, hold for seven seconds, and exhale slowly for eight seconds, making a "whoosh" sound as you breathe out. Repeat this cycle three to four times for each stretch. This will help you relax your muscles and mind, improving your recovery and flexibility.

Cool-down walks are good for recovery if you have been jogging or running. They help your body transition from a high-intensity workout to a resting state. Walking can also help prevent muscle stiffness and soreness by gradually reducing your heart rate and allowing your body to return to its normal state. To get the best out of your cool-down walks, inhale deeply through your nose for three to four steps, then exhale slowly through your mouth for the next three to four steps. Continue this pattern for five to ten minutes or until you feel your heart rate has returned to normal.

If you feel uncomfortable when using any of these techniques, don't ignore your body. You can consult with your breath instructor, gym instructor, or doctor to devise a plan that works best for you.

Breathing Exercises for Body Systems and Organs

It is a common occurrence to ignore or suppress any signs of illness until our life force becomes trapped in prolonged contraction and we manifest with serious physiological malfunction. Over the past 35 years of my practice as a healer, I have observed that my clients, like you, have the ability to tell the story of why they fell sick, how long they've been feeling like that, which part of the body they think is affected, and how they sometimes didn't take the signs seriously until the problem became a concern they couldn't ignore.

This section will explore carefully structured exercises that help you connect with your body and use your breath to restore health by focusing on different body systems and organs. These exercises are not a substitute for treatment from your primary healthcare team but a supplement that will help you reach complete healing and wellness. Also, it is essential to connect your spiritual, emotional, and physical dimensions when facing health problems, as this helps you achieve a holistic approach to health.

As always, before starting any breathing exercises, find a quiet, comfortable place to lie down and relax without any distractions. If you would like to do so, play some calming music to bring a feeling of peace and healing. Next, close your eyes and concentrate on your natural breathing rhythm. Observe where your breath flows freely and where it feels constricted or tense.

Once you've settled into your breath, direct your attention to any tense or ailing areas in your body. The tense region might be a specific body organ or system experiencing discomfort or tension. Below is a step-by-step guide on breathing and healing your organs to health.

Breathe In Love, Breathe Out What Emerges

In the previous chapter, we looked at how you can breathe out trauma and contraction, replacing those feelings by breathing in love. In these exercises, you will follow the same pattern, except the core focus is on the affected physical organ or system that you feel is unwell. After identifying the affected area, breathe a sense of love, warmth, and compassion into the region of focus. Feel this love filling your body before you start breathing out. Attach all the tension, discomfort, or negative emotions to your breath as you exhale. Doing this helps you replenish your energy, healing and unblocking any energy pathways that have been stagnant and contributing to your unwellness. It's also important to note that during this process, don't try to force or control events; allow your breath to flow naturally as you observe your experience judgment-free.

Your body holds knowledge and memories of feelings that may be causing you to feel unwell. These memories may be unpleasant, but as you unlock them, ask yourself: What is this part of my body trying to tell me? Thinking in this way may help you uncover any emotions you've been holding that may manifest as a physical symptom.

Revitalize Through Breath

As you focus your breath on the desired body organ, breathe the life force energy into that body part. As you exhale, visualize releasing all the tension, stress, and other negative energy, which leaves your body with the expelled air. Feel the changes in your body as your breath creates new energy pathways and restores vitality.

Continue breathing while visualizing your breath, nourishing and rejuvenating every body organ. Let's take this a step further by targeting the specific body systems below:

Digestive System

With this system in mind, take a deep breath into your abdomen. Visualize this air passing through your stomach, intestines, and liver. As it cleanses its way through the digestive system, feel the improvement in your digestion and metabolism. As you inhale this healing energy, expel any tension or discomfort with your breath when exhaling.

Respiratory System

Your breath will focus on your chest, throat, lungs, and airways. As you breathe in, feel the expansion in your chest. Visualize this breath clearing out toxins and congestion inside the respiratory system, leaving your airways and lungs open and refreshed.

Circulatory System

To shift focus to the cardiovascular system, picture your breath circulating through your bloodstream to your heart. On a molecular level, imagine the oxygen being delivered to the cells in your blood, bringing vitality. As you exhale, releasing any stress you feel is restricting your blood flow with the air you breathe out.

Lymphatic System

This is a group of organs and circulatory vessels with channels throughout all body tissues. It functions as a drainage system that helps remove waste and toxins from the body's systems, helps fight diseases, and maintains fluid balance. A fault in this system may result in swelling in the abdomen or legs, pain in affected lymph node regions, fatigue, and compromised immune function. To cleanse and clear your lymphatic system, breathe in while imagining the lymph nodes around your body being stimulated. Feel the air carrying and flushing out these toxins, bringing balance to this system.

Endocrine System

The endocrine system is a network of glands that produce hormones that help govern our daily and physiological activities. These glands are located throughout the body, significantly regulating metabolism, growth, sexual function, and mood. First, focus on your breath as it travels to your glands, such as the thyroid in your throat or the adrenal glands on top of the kidneys. Visualize your breath, balancing the release of these hormones.

Reproductive System

You can breathe fresh energy into your reproductive organs during inhalation. As you breathe in, feel the air expanding from your lower abdomen to your pelvis. Picture the breath of life nourishing this system's functions, which include ovulation, menstruation, libido, and fertility in women and sperm production and libido function in men. As you breathe out, release any stored tension or emotional pain and let the life force move freely in this area.

Auditory and Visual Systems

To cleanse the organs responsible for your sight and hearing, as you inhale, imagine the breath of life reaching and cleansing your eyes, ears, and the visual cortex and temporal lobe in your brain. This breath will replenish your senses, allowing your vision and hearing to improve with each inhalation. During exhalation, release all the negative energy with your breath. Feel these systems getting unclogged and refreshed. Enjoy the flowing, vibrant energy and revitalize your auditory and visual systems.

Rest for several minutes when you feel enough healing energy is flowing through your body. Gradually bring your awareness back to your body and take a few deep, grounding breaths. Take a minute to be grateful for any insights or breakthroughs during the practice. Trust that your body is striving for balance and healing.

Consistently practicing this exercise will strengthen the connection between your mind, body, and spirit. By focusing on your breath and imagining energy flowing through your body's systems and organs, you help your body naturally heal, release tension, and restore vitality.

Mental and Emotional Health

In previous chapters, we have extensively discussed emotional health, including trauma, suppressed emotions, and their impact on behavior and breathing patterns. In this section, we will examine both mental and emotional health, with a particular emphasis on mental health. Although closely related, mental and emotional health are distinct aspects of well-being. Mental health concerns the state of your cognitive, behavioral, and psychological well-being. This includes how you think, process information, manage stress, and make decisions. Meanwhile, emotional health focuses on how you understand, manage, and express your emotions. This includes emotional awareness, regulation, and resilience.

Despite their differences, mental and emotional health have a direct connection and can impact each other's condition. Emotional distress, such as chronic stress, can lead to mental health challenges, such as anxiety or depression. On the other hand, mental health disorders often manifest through emotional symptoms such as mood swings or emotional numbness, as seen in major depressive disorders.

Aside from playing a part in how you think, feel, act, and handle stress, positive mental health is important for maintaining excellent physical health, building beautiful bonds, and enjoying your daily activities. Positive mental health also helps you thrive in academics, social settings, and management roles, boosting your resilience and your ability to thrive, make informed decisions, and manage emotions. Neglecting your mental health puts you at risk of developing emotional distress, distancing yourself in relationships, reducing productivity, and increasing the risk of physical illness.

Signs You're Not Okay

Both children and adults tend to display certain signs or behaviors when struggling with mental health. In this section, we will examine the common indicators that both children and adults may exhibit when their mental health requires attention. Please keep in mind that if you suspect or relate to any of the signs below, it's important to consult a mental health specialist before drawing any conclusions on your own.

Signs in Children

- Behavior changes: You may notice a significant shift in their typical attitude, such as a withdrawal from social interactions or an increase in aggression and frequent tantrums.

- Decline in academic performance: Consistently poor school performance or a lack of interest in learning could indicate underlying emotional or mental struggles.

- Difficulty concentrating: You may notice the child having difficulty focusing on tasks, or they may appear more daydreamy or distracted than they should.

- Sleep problems: Children may also experience changes in their sleep patterns, such as difficulty falling asleep, frequent nightmares, or an excessive desire to sleep.

- Appetite changes: You may notice a sudden decrease or increase in their appetite, which is typically accompanied by mood changes.

- Physical complaints: Children may also complain of frequent stomach aches and headaches without any medical cause, which could be a sign of emotional distress that is influenced by mental health or vice versa.

Signs in Adults

- Constant fatigue: You may be waking up feeling mentally or physically drained even after getting adequate rest. This can be an indication of mental burnout or depression.

- Persistent sadness: Feeling sad is normal, but it shouldn't be constant. Ongoing feelings of hopelessness or worry for more than two weeks may be a sign of an underlying mental health concern.

- Difficulty managing emotions: If you experience sudden mood swings, are easily irritable, or feel overwhelmed by emotions, it might be a sign that your mental health is not coping well and needs your attention.

- Loss of interest in activities: You may notice that you are no longer interested in your hobbies, work, or social activities.

- Changes in sleeping patterns: You may experience difficulty falling asleep, waking up in the night, or oversleeping, all of which indicate a mental strain.

- Increased substance use: You may find yourself turning to alcohol, drugs, or other harmful coping mechanisms to help relieve your stress or turn away from your emotions.

- Physical symptoms: Having unexplained body aches, headaches, or digestive problems that don't have an identifiable medical cause may stem from poor mental health.

- Social isolation: You might find yourself avoiding social situations, withdrawing from family or friends, or feeling disconnected from others, which can be a sign of poor mental health.

Misconceptions About Mental Health

Despite increased awareness of mental and emotional health in our time, there are still some misconceptions and biases that often stand in the way of some people, hindering them from seeking help. These misconceptions can influence your perception of mental health, others' judgment of you, and your approach to emotional challenges. Overcoming these biases is crucial to mental health, so we'll discuss them below.

One of the most common misconceptions is that mental health problems are a matter of choice, and that you can choose to snap out of it. This misconception may lead you to overlook your mental health struggles and discourage you from seeking help. In reality, mental health struggles such as trauma, anxiety, and depression have a complicated nature as they are shaped by several factors, including genes, surroundings, and life events. This shows that willpower alone is not enough to treat mental health, proving the need for empathy, understanding, and frequent expert support.

Another common misconception is that emotions such as sadness, anger, or anxiety are full of negativity and should be suppressed. This is a part of most people's upbringing, teaching us that expressing emotions is a sign of weakness. This may result in emotional suppression, which in turn traps negative emotions.

People of different races, cultures, and genders are also subject to widespread mental health biases. For instance, people often expect men to conceal their emotions, while they perceive women as overly sensitive. Some cultures may look down upon or even laugh at people with mental health problems.

Challenging these beliefs begins with education and open communication. When you question these prejudiced preconceptions, you can create empathy, understanding, and a more welcoming view of mental health struggles for yourself and your loved ones.

Reframing and Improving Mental Clarity

Reframing your mind can help improve mental clarity by challenging negative thoughts and replacing them with more positive and empowering beliefs. This may also help you to heal emotionally and manage cognitive tasks with greater ease and efficiency. In this section, we will focus on different exercises that will help you reframe your thoughts and improve mental clarity.

To begin, we will explore ways to open up your third-eye chakra, or Ajna. Recall that this chakra is the center of intuition, insight, and mental clarity. When this chakra is balanced and open, you can experience improved mental clarity, better decision-making, and an ability to see things from a broader perspective. This balance will also influence how you perceive reality, process information, and connect with your inner wisdom. Without further ado, let's look into these exercises.

Third-Eye Meditation

The power of meditation goes beyond relaxing your mind; it can activate and balance your third-eye chakra. The key to this practice is focusing on the area between your eyebrows, where the third eye is believed to reside. The following is a guide for a basic third-eye meditation exercise.

Find a peaceful, calm spot where you can avoid distractions. Position yourself comfortably, whether sitting cross-legged on a mat or upright in a chair with your feet flat on the floor. Next, take a few deep breaths to relax your body, then breathe in through your nose, pause for a second, and breathe out through your mouth. Repeat this until you notice your body and mind calming down. After that, shift your focus to between your eyebrows, where your third-eye chakra is located. Imagine a bright indigo or violet light being emitted from this spot. Imagine it growing brighter as you breathe in and radiate with each exhalation.

Next, chant a mantra such as "Om" or "Aum." As you chant, visualize the vibration spreading through your third eye; this will bring harmony and help you gain wisdom. Stay present with the sensation and divert any thoughts that might disturb you. After 10–15 minutes, slowly bring your attention back to your physical surroundings. Gradually open your eyes and take a few deep breaths as you close or repeat this session.

This meditation promotes clarity of reasoning, a calm mind, and inner peace. Regular practice can help you access intuitive wisdom and improve your mental well-being.

Mind and Body Energy Alignment

Grounding exercises help keep your energy field stable and prevent your intuitive thoughts from overwhelming you. This practice combines grounding and using the third eye to clear your mind.

Start by sitting comfortably with your feet flat on the ground, your spine aligned, and your palms resting on your thighs. Close your eyes and direct your attention to your breath. Visualize roots growing from the base of your spine into the Earth. As these roots extend deeper, you will feel a stronger connection to the Earth's core. As you inhale, feel the Earth's energy rising through your roots, nourishing your entire being.

Once you feel grounded, shift your focus to the area between your eyebrows. Imagine the energy from the Earth moving up through your body toward this point. As it reaches the third eye, visualize it lighting up the indigo or violet light there. As the energy strengthens, imagine a line connecting your third eye to your crown chakra (at the top of your head). This alignment promotes the easy flow of energy, improving your mental clarity and intuition.

After 10-15 minutes, slowly shift your focus back to the Earth's energy. Feel the energy settle in your body as you expel any surplus through your roots.

Spiral Breathing for Clarity and Focus

This exercise uses spiral visualizations to open and clean the third eye, helping to dissolve obstacles and restore clarity.

To start, keep your spine straight. Get in a seated position or lie on your back. Next, close your eyes and relax. Focus on your breath by breathing deeply through your nose and exhaling through your mouth. Now, imagine a spiral of light in the area of your third eye between your eyebrows.

As you breathe in, visualize how this spiral gradually expands outward. As you exhale, envision the spiral contracting back into your third eye. With each breath, allow the spiral to expand further, covering your forehead and then your entire head. As you breathe, you can feel the release of tension and the removal of blockages in your third eye.

As the spiral grows, deepen your breath, feeling your diaphragm expand fully. Visualize the spiral of light reaching up to your crown chakra and down through your throat chakra, clearing and aligning your energy field.

To complete the exercise, gently bring the spiral back to the center of your third eye after 10–20 minutes of practice. Take a deep, big breath one final time, and release any remaining tension as you breathe out. When you feel ready, open your eyes and return to the present moment. Taking care of your health benefits you by opening your channels to relationships and contributing positively to the world. In the next chapter, we will look into rational health, how emotions are connected, and how they impact global health.

Types of Yoga Breathing Techniques

Before we begin, let us clarify and clear the confusion between breathwork practices and breathwork techniques. Though closely related, these two serve different purposes and have quite different approaches. Breathwork practices consist of regular, structured sessions that focus on awareness to achieve deep, transformative, and lasting benefits. These practices are often holistic, aiming to improve your physical, emotional, and spiritual health over time.

On the other hand, breathwork techniques are specific, isolated exercises or methods of conscious breathing. These techniques, which we are going to look into next, are often taught and used as tools within a broader breathwork or meditation practice. Usually, the focus is on mastering specific breathing patterns, controls, or applications. Breathwork techniques aim to produce immediate results, such as mind relaxation, stress relief, or increased focus, while breathwork practices aim for long-term transformation.

Let's explore these techniques. Perhaps you will discover a few that appeal to your lifestyle.

Diaphragmatic Breathing

Often referred to as belly breathing, this basic technique focuses on deep breaths that aim to expand the diaphragm. It is highly effective for promoting relaxation, reducing stress, and improving lung efficiency.

- First, find a comfortable position; this can be sitting or lying down. Next, relax your body, keeping your shoulders loose. Rest one hand on your chest and the other on your abdomen.

- Gently and slowly breathe in through your nose, ensuring that your belly expands as the air fills your lungs. Remember to keep your chest relatively still.

- For four to six seconds, exhale slowly through your mouth. Your exhale time should be slightly longer than your inhalation, as this helps to promote relaxation. With your hand, you should feel your abdomen flatten as the air leaves your lungs. Again, your chest should move very little.

- Continue to inhale deeply and exhale slowly, focusing on the expansion and contraction of your abdomen. While maintaining slow and smooth breaths, keep your breathing consistent and controlled.

The duration of this simple exercise can range from five to ten minutes each day. As you advance from a beginner level, you can increase the duration to whatever you are more comfortable with.

Diaphragmatic breathing stimulates the parasympathetic nervous system, which helps to induce relaxation and alleviate stress. Furthermore, this technique helps improve lung efficiency due to the full lung expansion and improved oxygen exchange in your body.

Box Breathing

Also known as square breathing, this is a simple, effective technique that relies on inhaling, holding, exhaling, and holding your breath for equal counts of four seconds.

- Find a comfortable, quiet place where you can easily focus without distractions.

- As you start, breathe out all the air you currently have in your lungs.

- Breathe in slowly through your nose for a count of four seconds. Feel the oxygen pumping into your lungs.

- Next, hold your breath for a count of four while keeping your body relaxed and your mind calm.

- Exhale gradually through your mouth for four seconds. Feel the oxygen leaving your lungs as you breathe out.

- Now pause and hold your breath for another four seconds before starting the cycle again.

- Continue this pattern for several minutes until you feel more centered and calm.

You can use this technique in high-stress situations, such as the moments before a presentation, a challenging conversation, or any other stressful event. It helps your nervous system reduce anxiety and manage emotions.

You can also practice box breathing before bedtime to help calm your mind and prepare your body for a good night's rest. Additionally, this technique is helpful during meditation sessions because it helps you focus and improves the outcome.

Alternate Nostril Breathing

This is an ancient breathing technique that is used in yoga practices. This technique, also known as nadi shodhana or subtle energy-clearing breathing, involves alternating the flow of air as you breathe through each nostril. This exercise is popular due to its ability to balance the mind and body, promoting mental clarity and emotional stability.

- Start by sitting comfortably with a straight spine, relaxed shoulders, and crossed legs.

- Rest your left hand on your knee; use your right hand to manage your breathing. Use your right thumb and ring finger to close your nostrils.

- Take a deep breath in and out. Gently close your right nostril with your right thumb. Then, take a slow, deep breath through your left nostril, paying attention to the sensation of the air filling your lungs.

- Next, use your ring finger to close your left nostril while simultaneously releasing your right thumb from your right nostril. Breathe out slowly through your right nostril. Enjoy the feeling of the air leaving your lungs.

- Next, with your left nostril still closed, take a deep breath in through your right nostril and enjoy the air filling your lungs.

- Press your thumb against your right nostril to close it, then open your left nostril. Using your left nostril, slowly breathe out the air from your lungs.

- This concludes one complete cycle of alternate nostril breathing. Your session may last five to ten minutes or as long as you can comfortably manage.

- Take a few moments after each workout to reflect on your experience and how the exercise has impacted your mind and body.

Research confidently confirms that alternate nostril breathing enhances the performance of our brain hemispheres (Garg et al., 2016). Breathing through the left nostril benefits the right hemisphere, while breathing through the right nostril supports the left hemisphere. This improvement in hemisphere function leads to increased focus, concentration, and overall brain function.

Another important benefit of alternate nostril breathing is the ability to help you calm your nervous system; this will aid in reducing stress and anxiety.

Pursed-Lip Breathing

This simple but very effective technique helps you take charge of your breath by slowing it down intentionally. This technique enhances lung oxygenation, which is particularly advantageous for individuals with respiratory conditions like COPD.

- Sit in a comfortable place. Relax your upper body and maintain an upright posture. This posture will help you get the most out of the deep breathing.

- Take a deep, slow breath through your nose for two to four seconds. Feel the air moving from your chest to your abdomen.

- Purse your lips like a whistle before exhaling. This will help you control the exhalation due to airflow resistance. You can exhale for four to six seconds. Your exhalation should be longer than your inhalation because it helps expel all the stored air in your lungs.

- For safety reasons, your session should last five to ten minutes, and you should only take three to five breaths per minute.

- Pursed-lip breathing slows down the breathing rate, allowing more time for oxygen to enter the lungs and carbon dioxide to leave. This improves your lung function.

This technique helps make breathing easier, especially during physical activities such as walking or climbing stairs, by prolonging the breaths, which keeps the airways open longer. This is very helpful for people living with COPD.

Furthermore, controlled breathing reduces anxiety and helps you feel more confident about your breathing.

Kapalabhati (Skull Shining Breath)

Kapalabhati is an ancient, advanced yogic cleansing technique. Kapalabhati is a Sanskrit word that translates to skull-shining breath. It involves rapid, forceful exhalations followed by passive inhalations. It is well-known for its ability to cleanse your respiratory system, improve lung function, and improve mental clarity.

- As with every breathing exercise we have looked into, find a comfortable place and sit upright with your spine straight and shoulders relaxed. Place your hands on your knees, then turn your palms upward, facing the sky or ceiling.

- Next, take a deep breath through your nose and let it fill your lungs.

- Pull your abdomen back to your spine with some force to expel the air out of your lungs quickly.

- Now relax as you breathe automatically and naturally.

- If you are a beginner, start with short sessions of one to two minutes. Perform two to three rounds of ten to twenty breaths each. As you get used to it, you can extend the session duration to five to ten minutes and increase your breaths per round. Do not forget to listen to your body if you ever feel discomfort during the session. Also, rest for about thirty seconds to one minute between rounds.

Below are some benefits of practicing kapalabhati breathing.

- Aids in expelling stale air and toxins from the lungs, promoting optimal respiratory health.

- Increases blood circulation, which is good for your

cardiovascular health and all of your organs, because they get enough oxygen through the blood.

- Helps in burning belly fat and improving digestion by massaging the abdominal organs.

- Helps you clear your mind and improve your focus for any tasks ahead.

We have now explored advanced breathing techniques and the powerful force behind them, which can help bring life into your body, mind, and spirit. In the next chapter, we will explore the meaning of trauma, the role your brain plays in trauma processing, the types of trauma, and the healing options available to you.

Chapter 9:

Relationships and Community

Alone, we can do so little; together, we can do so much.
–Helen Keller

So far, we have covered emotional, mental, and physical health and how you can heal from built-up emotions, but being healthy doesn't stop with your own well-being. As the cosmos reveals that we are just a part of the larger universe, it's only suitable to look at relational and community health and how our emotions contribute to the environment. It is my insight that there is a tremendous amount of emotional pollution activated by all types of trauma, from abusive relationships to war, greed, pride, and caste systems in all cultures. This emotional pollution disrupts the balance of our environment as much as, or even more than, physical pollutants.

Emotional pollution, a term I use to describe the negative energy of unresolved emotional pain that we all carry, can profoundly affect our relationships and communities. Just as physical pollution can harm ecosystems, emotional pollution can disrupt our relationships, leading to conflict, mistrust, and a breakdown in our social function.

This chapter will explore how unresolved inner conflicts and emotions can influence our relationships and the world. We will also discuss how we can unite and heal through breathwork to strengthen our relationships and community health.

Inner Conflicts Affects on Relationships

Holding on to emotions that remind us of our trauma or unaddressed emotional pain affects our relationships with our loved ones and communities. These unaddressed emotions can manifest as psychological defense mechanisms as we interact with others. These defense mechanisms, which start as protective strategies, can eventually become obstacles, robbing us of a real connection with and understanding of our loved ones.

Psychological defense mechanisms are unconsciously learned strategies we use to protect ourselves from emotional pain or anxiety. While these mechanisms offer temporary relief, they often lead to cycles of hurt and misunderstanding in relationships. Knowing and overcoming these defense mechanisms can help mend or build our connections with others and spread positivity worldwide. Let's look into some of Sigmund Freud's psychological defense mechanisms.

Projection

Projection involves attributing your thoughts, feelings, or impulses to someone else. It's a way of avoiding uncomfortable truths about yourself by imagining that they belong to another person. Projection often arises as a result of unresolved emotions from childhood developmental stages or a fear of confronting your flaws or insecurities. For example, if you struggle with feelings of inadequacy, you might project them onto your partner, accusing them of not being supportive or loving enough.

Even though you might find comfort in shying away from your feelings, projection can cause misunderstandings and conflict within your relationships. It also creates a distorted view of the relationship, making it challenging to address the real problem. As a result, you will have a cycle of blame and defensiveness, eroding trust and intimacy. Reflecting on the unresolved memories and images can provide insight into this mechanism and provide the power to heal.

Denial

Denial is refusing to accept reality or the facts presented before you because it's not the truth you want to hear. This rejection of reality blocks your awareness of external events, leading to denial. These blockages may be due to fear, shame, or guilt. For example, you might be denying the impact of your partner's addiction on your relationship to avoid emotions of anger, disappointment, or fear.

This may prevent you from addressing the underlying problem in your relationship, giving it the chance to fester and grow. A continual state of denial may lead to a communication breakdown, unmet needs, and the gradual death of the relationship.

Repression

Unlike denial, where you consciously ignore reality, repression happens unconsciously. It involves the unconscious blocking of painful or uncomfortable thoughts, feelings, or memories from your conscious awareness.

These unconscious blockages may be a result of trauma or experiences that are too overwhelming for you to process. Repressed emotions and memories may resurface in relationships in unexpected ways, causing emotional outbursts, withdrawal, or unexplained anxiety and creating distance between you and your partner or other people you are close to.

Displacement

Have you ever had one of those days when you were angry at your boss but couldn't do anything about it, so you threw that tantrum at your family or colleagues? That is displacement, or redirecting your emotions or impulses from a threatening target to a safer one. Displacement happens when you are unable to express your emotions toward the source due to a fear of the consequences or social norms. Continuous displacement of emotions can create a cycle of misdirected anger or frustration in relationships, leading to avoidable conflict, tension, and damage.

Rationalization

Rationalization is creating plausible but false explanations to justify your unacceptable behavior just so you can avoid confronting the actual underlying reasons for your actions. For instance, you might rationalize abandoning a relationship because you think your partner is better off without you, when in fact you are afraid of commitment. Eventually, this can lead to a pattern of avoiding intimacy and vulnerability in future relationships. Rationalization often stems from a desire to maintain self-esteem or avoid guilt, leading you to escape responsibility for your actions, causing repeated dishonesty and self-deception, and hindering your personal growth and connections with others.

Unspoken Contracts in Relationships

Unspoken contracts in our relationships often operate without our conscious awareness, dictating how we expect others to behave toward us. In Light Emerging, Barbara Brennan explains that these contracts are unspoken agreements or expectations that we unconsciously hold about how relationships or a group should work (Brennan, 1993). There are two types of contracts: negative and positive ones. Healthy relationships are based on interdependence, mutual support, honesty, and care, allowing positive contracts to shine and encouraging personal growth, creativity, and freedom. In contrast, codependent relationships start from negative contracts that limit and control personal development in the relationship. Positive and negative contracts often form unconsciously and usually work automatically, influencing our behavior and responses without us even realizing it.

The Roots of Negative Contracts

The foundation of most negative contracts starts from childhood experiences or past traumas that may lead someone to seek validation and security in unhealthy ways. Let's take a mother-and-child relationship, for example. If a mother holds an unspoken contract that her child will always behave well and never disappoint her, the mother may feel hurt or angry when the child inevitably does something that falls short of those expectations. Instead of recognizing her unrealistic expectations, she may react defensively by blaming the child, distancing herself emotionally, or rebuking the child. In this case, the mother's defensive reaction is rooted in a negative contract, expecting the child to always meet her standards to preserve her sense of control or emotional safety.

In response, the child may grow up feeling like they need to earn their mother's love by being perfect; they may carry this negative contract into adulthood, thinking that to be loved they shouldn't make mistakes. As this child gets into relationships in adulthood, they may struggle with accepting their imperfections or feel devastated when others don't meet their expectations of perfection, triggering their defense mechanism.

Negative contracts like this trap us in old patterns of defensiveness, causing us to react based on past wounds rather than present reality. These patterns often lead to cycles of disappointment, hurt, and misunderstanding, making it challenging to build healthy relationships.

Relational Healing

Coming to terms with psychological defense mechanisms and recognizing how unspoken contracts shape our actions opens the door to healing and personal growth. In my experience, unveiling deep feelings of disappointment that trigger our defense mechanisms makes it easier to work through the different conflicts we hold. In my journey of disappointment, there were times when I could be so defensive due to letdowns from both internal and external factors. I decided to meditate for emotional relief, and while meditating, I heard a quiet voice whispering in my ear, saying, "Why do you think you should never be disappointed in life?" I stopped for a while and started reflecting on this.

In that moment, I saw how much pain from my childhood and adulthood was tied to the unrealistic expectations of perfection that I had. This made me question myself: "Can I surrender to this understanding and let love and grace guide me? Or will I keep repeating the same old patterns, holding onto pain and unmet expectations?" In that moment, I realized true healing is about embracing imperfections in myself and others.

One of the most important steps in experiencing healthier relationships is self-reflection. Self-reflection helps us open our hearts to identifying and breaking negative contracts that activate our defense mechanisms, which will help us build healthier connections with others. Exercises that target identifying your negative contracts and breaking free of them have their roots in Barbra Brennan's Light Emerging (Brennan, 1993). By the end of these exercises, you should be able to recognize specific patterns in complicated relationships and how you may contribute to healing.

Identifying and Breaking Negative Contracts

To begin, select a relationship where you often feel uncomfortable or act in ways that don't reflect your true self. Having identified the relationship, think of how you behave differently in this relationship compared to others where you feel more at ease. This exercise is suggested in Chapter 13 of Light Emerging by Brennan on how to create healthy relationships. She outlines how to identify and change the negative patterns.

What actions do you take that feel unnatural or forced? Write down your answers in your journal. Next, ask yourself why you feel compelled to act this way. What are you afraid might happen if you don't? Note down what you fear the other person will do or think. Continue breaking down your emotional walls by reflecting on whether your fear based actions likely come from a more profound belief about yourself and the world.

Write down what you believe you must do to control the other person's acceptance.

Now that you have found this unfavorable contract, write down the emotional and psychological cost of continuing this behavior. Write down how it affects other areas of your life. Finally, consider the overall cost of this unspoken negative contract to your well-being, growth, and happiness. When you are done with this we can move on to breaking these contracts. Let's look at the steps below:

1. In your journal, write down what you believe may happen to the relationship if you change your negative contract.

2. Take true action and observe the true result. For example, if you are uncomfortable about something in a relationship but don't say so because you fear you might start an argument, gather up your courage and express yourself. Then observe: Did the feared consequence occur? Or did something unexpected happen? You can go back to your journal and record the outcome.

3. Meditate on your new-found courage to not do something out of fear and disappointment but instead to communicate openly and honestly to strengthen the relationship.

4. Think of all the positivity and healthy boundaries you will create once you break this contract. Write down these potential improvements in your relationships with others around you.

Breathing Into Intimacy

We share intimate relationships with our life partners, family, and friends. These relationships are built on trust, vulnerability, and emotional connection. One way to re-establish our connections after discovering and freeing ourselves from a negative relationship contract is through breathwork. Breathwork has the potential to rekindle the light in your emotional connections and improve intimacy with your loved ones by aligning your breath, mind, and emotions. Let's look into some of the breathwork exercises that can help you and your loved ones strengthen your relationships and synchronize your breath and energy.

Eye-Gazing With Synchronized Heart Breathing

Eye-gazing and synchronizing our heartbeat with others is fundamental to relational health, thriving and wellbeing. We can change our emotions from uncomfortable to positive through breathwork. For this reason, we will use a physical approach to embrace love and synchronize your breath with your loved one so you can share the intimacy.

Listening to your partner's or loved one's heartbeat while breathing at the same time can unlock emotions you haven't felt in a while or bring a feeling of love all over again. This exercise helps you create a deeper emotional connection and intimacy with your partner by synchronizing your breath and engaging with your hearts. Follow these simple steps to experience a powerful bond:

1. Find a quiet, comfortable space where you and your partner

can sit facing each other, either cross-legged on the floor or in chairs. Make sure you both feel relaxed and at ease.

2. Sit comfortably and make direct eye contact with your partner. Let your eyes meet and stay focused on each other. Allow yourselves to be open and present with one another, letting go of any distractions.

3. Once you have established eye contact, begin to synchronize your breathing with your partner. Inhale and exhale together, matching each other's rhythm. Focus on the feeling of breathing in unison, and let that create a sense of unity and connection.

4. While still gazing into each other's eyes and breathing together, gently place one hand on your heart and the other hand on your partner's heart. Both of you should do this. This will help you connect even more deeply.

5. Now, focus on your heartbeats. As you continue to breathe deeply, imagine a warm, glowing light in your heart. Visualize this light spreading throughout your body and extending to your partner's heart, creating a shared energy between you both.

6. Continue breathing deeply, keeping your focus on the energy between your hearts. Allow the warmth and love to grow as your hearts beat in sync, creating a powerful connection.

7. After several minutes, slowly bring the exercise to a close. Take a moment to reflect on the connection you've shared. Sit together in silence, appreciating the bond you've just nurtured.

Repeat this exercise whenever you want to deepen your intimacy and strengthen your relationship. Over time, it will help you feel more connected, loving, and united.

Breathwork for Conflict Resolution

Emotions can run high during conflicts, leading to impulsive reactions and communication breakdowns. The good news is that breathwork can help you stay centered and open-minded, reducing the likelihood of regrettable heated arguments. In this section, we will use breathwork to cool down your nervous system and promote relaxation, giving you room for reason and thoughtful conflict resolution skills.

Below are some exercises that can help calm your emotions during conflict situations.

Energetic Reconciliation

This exercise requires a hands-on, energetic technique that is highly effective in any disagreement or painful interaction. We usually apply this simple seven-step technique at the Brennan School of Healing when training our students, but you can also easily follow it below:

1. Take a moment to pause and identify your reaction. Are you fleeing, collapsing, withholding, combusting in anger, or denying the matter? This step is crucial in understanding how you're emotionally or energetically responding to the

situation.

2. Once you've realized how reactive you are, take a pause from participating in the conversation. Avoid saying or doing anything that fuels the conflict further.

3. Visualize cutting the energy flow you are experiencing so you no longer feel entangled in the emotional intensity. This will allow you to drop your energetic connection with the other person and regain clarity.

4. Let go of the emotions and thoughts you've been projecting onto the other person. Releasing this attachment frees you from the need to control the situation or expect a particular outcome.

5. Take a moment to turn inward and identify where your reaction is coming from. Are you feeling disappointed? Are you afraid of being abandoned or controlled? Do you need to be seen as perfect, or do you fear vulnerability? This introspection helps you find the root of your reactivity and improves your self-awareness.

6. Next, take several deep, full breaths to ground yourself, promoting balance in your energy and bringing inward focus and calmness. If you've been practicing the breathing exercises from earlier chapters, this step will be more intuitive.

7. Once you've centered yourself, you can choose how to proceed. Either continue the conversation from a calm and grounded place, or ask for a break and agree to revisit the discussion later when both parties feel more settled.

During an argument, you can ask your loved one to breathe with you when your emotions are spiraling out of control. Sit in a comfortable place; you can take a few deep breaths to cool down. Purse your lips and breathe through your mouth; feel the air reach your lungs, bringing in that calmness. Next, close your mouth and exhale slowly through your nose. Continue this breathing pattern for several minutes as you feel the air calming your body and mind. Over time, you will feel reduced anger and frustration toward your loved one and be more open to constructive dialogue.

You can also add compassion breathing as a way to awaken empathy and understanding toward yourself and the other person. This allows you to assess a situation without bias or judgment, and improve your conscious communication and decision-making.

Before entering a discussion to resolve a disagreement, take a few minutes to practice compassion breathing. Find a quiet place where you can focus on your breath. Breathe in empathy and understanding and release frustration and misunderstanding with every exhale. Continue doing this for a few minutes, and feel empathy and transparency inside you. Repeating this exercise will help you to de-escalate tensions and create a more supportive environment for resolving conflicts.

Breathwork for Communication

Effective communication is the foundation of healthy relationships. It allows open and honest expression of thoughts and feelings. It also helps you process any unspoken contracts or defense mechanisms you may have deployed. By using breathwork, you can improve your communication skills, creating clarity, patience, and empathy in your relationships. Let's look into some exercises that can help you with effective communication.

Illuminating Your Throat Chakra

Getting the confidence to speak your mind starts with clearing your throat chakra for complete confidence to communicate comfortably. To get started, find a comfortable position and sit with your spine straight as you gently place your hand on your throat. Imagine your throat area and chakra center open and clear.

You may want to use a mantra to open this area. One that I use, is "I speak truth from the I AM that I AM". I sit quietly and focus my breath to open my abdomen first, then open the diaphragm, allowing the breath to move up into the throat chakra. After breathing for a few minutes, repeat the mantra a few times. You may hear in your mind the justification of why you are right and the other is wrong. Breathe through these thoughts until you are able to hear a deeper sense of knowing and truth. What do you need to say from a peaceful non-reactive space? Can you hear the other? Lets review the steps:

1. Breathing in a cool blue light, allow the energy to start flowing without any hindrances. Imagine your throat area and chakra center open and clear.

2. You may want to repeat the mantra: "I speak truth from the I AM that I AM".

3. Sit quietly and focus your breath to open the abdomen first, then open the diaphragm, then allow the breath to move up into the throat chakra.

4. Next, inhale a few breaths while imagining a cool blue light entering your throat, clearing away any blockages or tension. As you breathe out, imagine this light radiating outward, clearing your throat and enabling you to speak clearly and confidently. Repeat until your throat feels clear.

5. After clearing with the blue light you may want to continue by repeating the mantra a few times.

6. Practice mindful awareness. You may hear justifications of why you are right and the other is wrong. Breathe through these thoughts until you are able to hear a deeper sense of listening to your inner wisdom and being in contact with the other person. What do you need to say from a peaceful non-reactive space? Can you hear the other?

7. Practice taking conscious breathing breaks during the conversations. This may prevent impulsive reactions. During pauses, mindful breathing helps you communicate in a self-regulated and thoughtful manner. It enables you to be an active listener, comprehending what the other person is saying as you breathe before responding.

During the conversation, breathe in slowly and fully before answering a question. As you breathe, gather your thoughts around the discussion, pay attention to how your body is responding, and decide how you want to respond.

Breathing Into Your Heart Chakra

In Chapter 3, we looked at the chakras; the heart chakra, or Anahata, is one of them. The heart chakra is responsible for centering love, compassion, and connection. An unbalanced heart chakra may lead to feelings of not loving yourself enough, which can obstruct you from loving those around you. You might express these emotions through insecurities and fear of being left. When balanced correctly, the heart chakra attracts the free flow of love and self-worth, helping you build healthy relationships. Let's look into some breathwork exercises that help improve the flow of energy through the heart chakra.

Heart-Centered Breathing

Practice Heart-Centered breathing by creating a sacred space for you to sit and relax.

1. Place your hands over your heart while you breathe in. With each inhale and exhale, notice how the air fills your chest and energy moves into your heart center. As you breathe in, visualize a green light radiating from your heart, growing brighter with each inhale. This light represents love, compassion, and healing energy flowing through you.

2. As you exhale, imagine this light spreading outward, covering your whole body and extending to those around you. Upon exhaling you may sense some stress or held emotions allowing those feelings, thoughts or experiences to be released until both the inhale and exhale radiates an emerald green.

3. Repeat this practice for five to ten minutes.

With practice, this exercise will aid in opening and balancing the heart chakra, which promotes the release of emotional blockages that may be preventing you from creating healthy and happy relationships.

Loving-Kindness Meditation With Breath

Cultivate loving kindness in all your relationships by practicing the Buddhist practice of Metta (which means loving kindness) meditation. This meditation combines breathwork with affirmation to cultivate compassion, kindness, and love for yourself and others.

1. Return to your sacred space to practice. Take a few deep breaths and slowly exhale to center yourself. Give yourself time to center yourself.

2. As you breathe deeply, silently repeat loving-kindness phrases, such as: "May I be happy, may I be healthy, may I be safe, may I live with ease". After a few minutes of repeating these phrases, extend these wishes to your loved ones by speaking positivity into their lives.

3. Next, you can extend these words to your colleagues, and later to someone you have challenges with. Picture your breath sending out your thoughts of kindness.

4. Consistent practice will help cultivate an open and loving heart and improve your ability to bond with and care for others.

By paying attention to your breath, you can create harmony and flow in all of your relationships. Take time each day to breathe into your heart the incredible bonds you share with others. Open your heart to the inner wisdom of your soul and replenish your life force with synchronizing your life pulse with the cosmos.

Community and Global Healing

As we live, each person's emotions and actions, whether positive or negative, can affect our communities and the global environment. In this section, we will explore how our actions can change a timeline of events that can lead to positive or negative outcomes. We will briefly look into how our collectiveness connects to the Earth and how we can use breathwork for our community and global emotional health, which can reduce emotional pollution.

It's important to acknowledge that personal insecurities, if left unaddressed, can snowball into significant societal problems. Wars, environmental degradation, and social injustices often stem from unresolved emotional wounds and fears within individuals or groups. History bears witness to the fact that many large-scale conflicts originate from personal or community insecurities that were not properly dealt with, leading to their escalation into violence and war.

On the other hand, when we come together, guided by love, compassion, and mutual respect, we can transform our communities and the world. Positive relationships built on empathy and understanding create a ripple effect that can heal divisions, inspire cooperation, and promote global peace. When we work together for the common good, we encourage others to do the same, leading to a worldwide movement toward peace, sustainability, and well-being.

Our Connection With the Earth

Having peace and understanding helps us care for our environment and planet, as this opens our awareness of all living beings and the importance of preserving our natural resources for future generations. We have a responsibility to look after our environment due to the interconnectedness we have with it.

The evidence is seen in scientific results showing that our bodies are 60% composed of water, and so is our planet, which is mainly covered in water (Sissons, 2020). A scientific study by Dr. Masaru Emoto further demonstrated how we are connected to nature as he experimented with the effects of emotions on water. During his research, he noted that positive thoughts, words, and music led to beautiful, well-formed ice crystals, while negative emotions or harsh words resulted in distorted, chaotic crystal formations (Archdall, 2023). Another recent example of how our collective existence can affect the Earth came from a Taylor Swift concert, where the crowd's energy caused the ground to shake in a phenomenon known as a "Swift quake." This phenomenon highlights the interconnectedness between human emotions and the environment (Che, 2023). These events remind us of our collective energy's impact on the world around us.

Now that we know that we achieve more together than alone, let's participate in some breathwork that can help create community, global healing, and a spirit of oneness.

Collective Breathing

Coming together and participating in collective breathwork can promote community-based connection and healing among us. Collective breathwork is when you gather as a group or community and breathe in synchrony. The shared connection in this synchrony can mature into a feeling of unity and belonging. Additionally, it improves trust, communication, and collaboration within communities and professional spaces, bringing innovation and mutual support.

There are many types of collective breathwork exercises. Here, we will briefly describe two popular workouts: synchronized group breathing and community breath circles.

Synchronized Group Breathing

Under the guidance of a skilled facilitator, you will be seated in a circle or gathered as a group, ensuring everyone can see and hear each other. The facilitator will lead you through a series of synchronized breathing patterns, such as box breathing or 4–7–8 breathing, to create a sense of unity and connection within the group.

Synchronized breathing harnesses the group's energies, creating a strong sense of belonging and shared purpose. If you're drawn to the idea of a collective group, start by exploring local classes, workshops, or online sessions led by certified breathwork facilitators. As you try different sessions, you'll find yourself immersed in a supportive community, breathing in unison with other participants.

To organize your session with family, friends, and other like-minded people, you should identify a trained breathwork coach and select a comfortable venue. Create a favorable schedule for everyone who is coming together for this transformative experience. Your instructor will guide all participants in setting an expected outcome for the session and provide other necessary guidance to ensure a safe and effective practice. Your facilitator will then guide you with breathwork techniques that align with your intention. At the end of the session, you will experience collective relaxation and connection as you reflect on the experience together. Your coach may also allow time for sharing and processing after the session to further strengthen participant bonds.

Community Gatherings

Community rituals might seem simple, but they carry emotional value and promote healing and unity within a group or community. They offer a vital opportunity for individuals to come together and actively support one another. You can also include breathwork practices in many different situations from religious gatherings, business meetings, healing circles or prayer groups. You can use this as an icebreaker for your gathering to create connection and bring the group into coherence. Often when people meet each individual brings energy from their experiences and it can be helpful to take some time to focus energy on what's present here and now.

There are a couple of ways through which you can participate in these rituals without spending more time or resources than you can afford. One way to do this is through monthly breathwork gatherings within your community. You and other community members may organize monthly meetings where members come together to practice breathwork and share their experiences. These gatherings can be a regular check-in, helping participants stay connected and supported. This also creates an opportunity for you to create community with others who are aware of the divine spark within them. As iron sharpens iron, these gatherings can encourage you to bring to life the potential that is within your core star.

Some of the activities you can try with your circle include candle light breath circles and breath gratitude ceremonies. For candlelight breath circles, in the evening, use candles to set a peaceful mood and create a calming and reflective atmosphere through breath circles. Participants can focus on the flame as they breathe, symbolizing the light and warmth they bring to each other's lives and the light that flows from the core star. For breath and gratitude ceremonies, during these ceremonies, you and the others can take turns sharing what you are grateful for, followed by collective breathing exercises. This ritual reinforces positive energy and strengthens the bonds within the community.

Through these activities, and all the others we have looked at in the book, we have extensively appreciated the cosmic act of breathing. When shared collectively, this can heal us individually and in our communities, bringing positivity to our planet. Adopting cosmic breathing in our everyday routine contributes to a sense of interconnectedness with the world around us, which helps bring peace.

Conclusion

As we come to the end of this exploration of the transformative power of breath, it's clear that breathing is far more than a biological function; it is a gateway to better understanding, healing, and connection. We have covered how breath acts as a bridge between our physical, emotional, and spiritual selves, showing us the potential for growth and self-discovery.

By now, you should know the historical, cultural, spiritual, and scientific perspectives of breath. These views uncovered how breath is sacred across different cultures as a source of life and a pathway to spiritual growth. This universal connection across time shows that we are part of a more significant force bound together by breath, which sustains all life forms.

We then examined the respiratory anatomy of the human body to understand how air travels in our bodies and its significance. We also looked into the metaphysical body, exploring the anatomy of our chakras and human energy consciousness system. This provided us with a better understanding of the vital role of breath, laying the groundwork for further exploration of the therapeutic potential of advanced breathwork techniques.

Regarding trauma, we discussed its relationship with breath

and how the brain processes trauma. From there, we connected trauma to character analysis—how our unconscious mind and early childhood experiences may shape our personalities and character, and how these events persist into adulthood, shaping our behavior and personality. We then introduced the concept of the life pulse, its cycle, and how its free flow promotes vitality and emotional openness. When obstructed by trauma, it results in a feeling of disconnect from ourselves. We also looked at how the life pulse can bring out the best of our core qualities when we nurture it properly.

We also explored how childhood trauma caused by neglect, abuse, or loss can disrupt emotional and psychological growth, leading to rigid defense mechanisms and personality patterns that limit emotional expression and intimacy. Through the work of Sigmund Freud, Wilhelm Reich, Alexander Lowen, Barbara Brennan, and Ronald Robbins, we appreciated how different personality patterns manifest in our bodies and energy fields. This gave us a foundation for recognizing how tension is built and how it influences our self-perception and interactions with others.

We covered how prolonged exposure to stress, anxiety, and trauma can lead to contracted breathing. These habitual, restricted breathing patterns reflect our unresolved tensions and have various implications, such as decreased oxygen flow to the brain and muscles, contributing to fatigue and tension. We shared different breath exercises to release trauma and contractions that block the natural flow of life force energy.

This guide also discussed the importance of maintaining our physical and emotional health and how the life force energy thrives better when we take care of ourselves. In the closing chapter, we moved from personal health to relationships and community health. We discovered that unresolved inner conflict could have a ripple effect on how we treat or respond to others. We also explored how breathwork can bring relational unity and help handle disputes. We further investigated the interconnectedness of all emotions in our universe, finding that negative emotions can lead to war, greed, and violence. However, through collective breathwork, we can promote healing, harmony, and positive change across the globe.

If you're still seeking the full benefits of breathwork, you may want to contact a Breathwork practitioner or a Brennan practitioner.

In my other books, I explore additional aspects of our divine and wonderful existence, and they all connect to the cosmic breath which you have now come to understand. You can find these books and other resources through my website www. donnaevansstrauss.com.

Breathing continues until we move to the next life; why not breathe in a way that heals, grows, and makes a difference in your life and the world!

About the Author

Donna Evans Strauss is an educator, Brennan Healing Science Facilitator, and author with over 35 years of experience in transpersonal psychology and energy healing. She has guided countless students as a senior faculty member and former Department Head of Brennan Healing Science. Donna designed and implemented the two-year Advanced Studies Brennan Integrative Work (ASBIW) program, a project demonstrating her excellence. For over 24 years, this program has trained facilitators, group leaders, and practitioners in Brennan Healing Science. Her expertise in the human energy consciousness system and healing has made her a sought-after speaker at international conferences and a trusted mentor in the healing community. In this groundbreaking book, she invites readers to explore the profound connections between cosmic breath, health, and the human biofield.

Other Book by Donna Evans Strauss

1. The Divine Genogram
2. Explore the Mysteries of the Cosmos ESP and the Human Biofield
3. Blessings From a Thousand Generations
4. Infinite Grace *(forthcoming)*

www.donnaevansstrauss.com

References

Ahuja, N. (2023, December 12). Breath, mind, and spirit—power of pranayama for well-being. Ayurveda Awareness Centre. https://www.ayurveda-awareness. com.au/breath-mind-and-spirit-power-of-pranayama-for-well-being/

American Heart Association. (n.d.). American Heart Association recommendations for physical activity in adults and kids. https://www.heart.org/en/ healthy-living/fitness/fitness-basics/aha-recs-for-physical-activity-in-adults

American Lung Association. (2017, July 19). How your lungs get the job done. https://www.lung.org/blog/how-your-lungs-work

American Psychiatric Association. (2013). Diagnostic and statistical manual of mental disorders (5th ed.). American Psychiatric Publishing.

Archdall, R. (2023, January 21). Water, thoughts and emotions: The effect on water. My Water Filter. https://mywaterfilter. com.au/blogs/learning/how-water-responds-to-thoughts-and-emotions

Atsma, A. J. (n.d.). Prometheus. The Theoi Project. https://www. theoi.com/Titan/ TitanPrometheus.html

Barrett Browning, E. Quote. In Agyei, S. (2016a, April 6). "He lives most life whoever breathes most air." Medium. https:// medium.com/@steveagyeibeyondlifestyle/he-lives-most-life-whoever-breathes-most-air-5eb0857fe64f

Brennan, B. A. (1990). Hands of Light: A guide to healing through the human energy field. Bantam.

Brennan, B. A. (1993). Light emerging. Bantam.

Brennan, B. A. (2017). Core light healing. Hay House, Inc.

Brenner, G. H. (2019, January 16). How yoga and breathing help the brain unwind. Psychology Today. https://www.psychologytoday.com/intl/blog/psychiatry-the-people/201901/how-yoga-and-breathing-help-the-brain-unwind

Buchanan, T. W., & Lovallo, W. R. (2019). The role of genetics in stress effects on health and addiction. Current Opinion in Psychology, 27, 72–76. https://doi. org/10.1016/j.copsyc.2018.09.005

Campbell, A. A., Wisco, B. E., Silvia, P. J., & Gay, N. G. (2019). Resting respiratory sinus arrhythmia and posttraumatic stress disorder: A meta-analysis. Biological Psychology, 144, 125–135. https://doi.org/10.1016/j.biopsycho.2019.02.005

Carlyle, T (n.d). Quote. In Twinkle. (2024, April 8). Happy World Health Day 2024: Quotes, wishes, slogans and captions to share with friends and family. Jagran Josh. https://www.jagranjosh.com/general-knowledge/happyworld-health-day-2024-wishes-quotes-slogans-captions-1712509264-1

Che, C. (2023, July 28). 'Swift quake': Taylor Swift fans shake ground during Seattle concert. The New York Times. https://www.nytimes.com/2023/07/28/arts/ music/taylor-swift-earthquake-seattle-.html

Cherry, K. (2023, February 22). What is attachment theory? Verywell Mind. https:// www.verywellmind.com/what-is-attachment-theory-2795337

Chourpiliadis, C., & Bhardwaj, A. (2022). Physiology, respiratory rate. StatPearls Publishing. https://www.ncbi.nlm.nih.gov/books/NBK537306/

Currivan, J. (2017). The cosmic hologram: In-formation at the center of creation. Simon & Schuster.

Davies, V. (2018). Peace in Ancient Egypt. Brill.

DeAngelis, T. (2023, December 5). War's enduring legacy: How does trauma haunt future generations? American Psychological Assoication. https://www.apa. org/topics/trauma/trauma-survivors-generations

Dillard, C. C., Martaindale, H., Hunter, S. D., & McAllister, M. J. (2023). Slow breathing reduces biomarkers of stress in response to a virtual reality active shooter training drill. Healthcare, 11(16), 2351. https://doi.org/10.3390/healthcare11162351

Egberts, J. (2023, May 4). The history of breathwork: Origins of this ancient healing practice. Breathless. https://breathlessexpeditions.com/origins-history-of-breathwork/

Farghaly, A., Fitzsimons, D., Bradley, J., Sedhom, M., & Atef, H. (2022). The need for breathing training techniques: The elephant in the heart failure cardiac rehabilitation room: A randomized controlled trial. International Journal of Environmental Research and Public Health, 19(22), 14694. https://doi. org/10.3390/ijerph192214694

Fincham, G. W., Kartar, A., Uthaug, M. V., Anderson, B., Hall, L., Nagai, Y., Critchley, H., & Colasanti, A. (2023). High ventilation breathwork practices: An overview of their effects, mechanisms, and considerations for clinical applications. Neuroscience and Biobehavioral Reviews, 155, 105453. https://doi. org/10.1016/j.neubiorev.2023.105453

Fortier, C. (2022, September 30). What is holotropic breathwork and how does it work? Fullscript. https://fullscript.com/blog/holotropic-breathwork

Freud, S. (1999). Die traumdeutung. [1], [reprint d. ausg. leipzig und wien 1899]. Fischer.

Garbarino, S., Lanteri, P., Bragazzi, N. L., Magnavita, N., & Scoditti, E. (2021). Role of sleep deprivation in immune-related disease risk and outcomes. Communications Biology, 4, 1304 (2021). https://doi.org/10.1038/s42003-02102825-4

Garg, R., Malhotra, V., Tripathi, Y., & Agarawal, R. (2016). Effect of left, right and alternate nostril breathing on verbal and spatial memory. Journal of Clinical and Diagnostic Research, 10(2), CC01–CC03. https://doi.org/10.7860/jcdr/2016/12361.7197

Hebert, S. (2012, December 4). The importance of proper breathing in managing chronic pain. MSU Extension. https://www.canr.msu.edu/news/the_importance_of_proper_breathing_in_managing_chronic_pain

Heim, M. A., & Makuch, M. Y. (2023). Breathing techniques during labor: A multinational narrative review of efficacy. The Journal of Perinatal Education,

32(1), 23–34. https://doi.org/10.1891/jpe-2021-0029

Holmes, S. W., Morris, R., Clance, P. R., & Putney, R. T. (1996). Holotropic breathwork: An experiential approach to psychotherapy. Psychotherapy: Theory,

Research, Practice, Training, 33(1), 114–120. https://doi.org/10.1037/00333204.33.1.114

The Holy Bible, New King James Version. (1982). Thomas Nelson.

Hu Fuchen. (2013). General theory of taoism. Paths International Ltd.

Invitto, S., & Moselli, P. (2024). Exploring embodied and bioenergetic approaches in trauma therapy: Observing somatic experience and olfactory memory. Brain Sciences, 14(4), 385. https://doi.org/10.3390/brainsci14040385

Jain, S. (2016). Effect of 6 weeks Kapalabhati pranayama training on pulmonary and cardiovascular parameters of young, prehypertensive obese medical students. International Journal of Medical Science and Public Health, 5(4),

1471–1474. https://doi.org/10.5455/ijmsph.2016.23102015233

James, W. (n.d.). William James quotes. QuoteFancy. https://quotefancy.com/ quote/934662/William-James-Tension-is-a-habit-Relaxing-is-a-habit-Badhabits-can-be-broken-good-habits

Keller, H. (n.d.). Quote. In Fisher, M. (2023, October 25). Alone we can do so little, together we can do so much—Helen Keller. Medium. https://fishouthebox. medium.com/alone-we-can-do-so-little-together-we-can-do-so-much-helen-keller-4db02c026a2e

Kessler, S., & Chrisman, C. (2015). The 5 personality patterns : Your guide to understanding yourself and others and developing emotional maturity. Bodhi Tree Press.

Laozi, & Chu, D. (1982). Dao de jing. Unwin Paperbacks.

Leonard, J., & Laut, P. (1991). Vivation. Vivation Publishing Company.

Lowen, A. (2012). The language of the body. Simon and Schuster.

Lowen, A. (2013). The spirituality of the body: Bioenergetics for grace and harmony. Bioenergetics Press.

Ma, X., Yue, Z.-Q., Gong, Z.-Q., Zhang, H., Duan, N.-Y., Shi, Y.-T., Wei, G.-X., & Li, Y.-F. (2017). The effect of diaphragmatic breathing on attention, negative affect and stress in healthy adults. Frontiers in Psychology, 8, 874. https://doi. org/10.3389/fpsyg.2017.00874

McCarty, N. A. (2021). Breathe—your immune system is counting on it. Journal of Experimental Medicine, 218(4), e20202643. https://doi.org/10.1084/ jem.20202643

Maté, G. Quote. In Bramley, E. V. (2023, April 12). The trauma doctor: Gabor Maté on happiness, hope and how to heal our deepest wounds. The Guardian. https://www.theguardian.com/lifeandstyle/2023/apr/12/the-trauma-doctor-gabor-mate-on-happiness-hope-and-how-to-heal-our-deepest-wounds

Miller, T., & Nielsen, L. (2015). Measure of significance of holotropic breathwork in the development of self-awareness. The Journal of Alternative and Complementary Medicine, 21(12), 796–803. https://doi.org/10.1089/acm.2014.0297

Naqshbandi principle: Awareness of breath(Hosh dar dam). (2014, December 9). Naqshabandi -Rabbani Way. https://naqshabandi.org/2014/12/09/naqshbandi-principle-awareness-of-breathhosh-dar-dam/

Nhat Hahn, T. (n.d.). Quote. In Kornbluth, J. (2023, October 17). "Breathing in, I calm my body. breathing out, I smile. dwelling in the present moment, I know this is a wonderful moment." Headbutler. https://headbutler.com/ reviews/thich-nhat-hanh-1926-2022-breathing-in-i-calm-my-body-breathing-out-i-smile-dwelling-in-the-present-moment-i-know-this-is-a-wonderful-moment/

The Noble Quran (M. Taqi-ud-Din al-Hilali & M. Muhsin Khan, Trans.). (1997). King Fahd Complex for the Printing of the Holy Qur'an. (Original work published n.d.)

Ohnishi, T., & Ohnishi, T. (2006). The Nishino breathing method and ki-energy (life-energy): A challenge to traditional scientific thinking. Evidence-Based Complementary and Alternative Medicine, 3, 324525. https://doi. org/10.1093/ecam/nel004

Patel, S., & Sharma, S. (2023). Respiratory acidosis. StatPearls Publishing. https:// www.ncbi.nlm.nih.gov/books/NBK482430/

Patterson, M. L. (2021, January 5). The air they breathed. Tales From the Two Lands. https://talesfromthetwolands. org/2021/01/05/the-air-they-breathed/

Patterson, N. (2022, January 13). Why self-care is important to your mental health. Medium. https://medium. com/@niapatterson/why-self-care-is-arguablythe-most-important-facet-of-your-mental-health-93f86494c694

Pfost, P. (2001). The Barbara Brennan school of healing and Brennan Healing Science. Complementary Health Practice Review, 7(2), 133–136. https://doi. org/10.1177/153321010100700207

Phillips, S. (2009). Yoga, karma, and rebirth: A brief history and philosophy. Columbia University Press.

Plato. (n.d.). Quote. In Whole Health Clinic. (2012, March 25). The part can never be well unless the whole is well. https://drsharif.com/the-part-can-never-bewell-unless-the-whole-is-well/

Pierrakos, J. C. (1987). Core energetics. Life Rhythm.

Porchon-Lynch, T. (n.d). Quote. In Vallejo, M. (2023, December 11). 60 best stress quotes for inner calm. Mental Health Center Kids. https://mentalhealthcenterkids.com/blogs/ articles/quotes-about-stress

Ramacharaka, Y. (2013). The Hindu-Yogi science of breath: A complete manual of the oriental breathing philosophy of physical, mental, psychic and spiritual development. YOGebooks. (Original work published 1903)

Ramos, E. M. C., Vanderlei, L. C. M., Ramos, D., Teixeira, L. M., Pitta, F., & Veloso, M. (2009). Influence of pursed-lip breathing on heart rate variability and cardiorespiratory parameters in subjects with chronic obstructive pulmonary disease (COPD). Brazilian Journal of Physical Therapy, 13(4), 288–293. https://doi.org/10.1590/s1413-35552009005000035

Reich, W. (2023). Character analysis. WRM Press.

Rink, C., & Khanna, S. (2011). Significance of brain tissue oxygenation and the arachidonic acid cascade in stroke. Antioxidants & Redox Signaling, 14(10), 1889–1903. https://doi.org/10.1089/ars.2010.3474

Robbins, R. (1990). Rhythmic integration: Finding wholeness in the cycle of change. Barrytown/Station Hill Press.

Roosevelt, T. (n.d). Quote. In Buckenmaier, C., III. (2020, June 8). The more you know about the past, the better prepared you are for the future. U.S. Medicine. https://www.usmedicine.com/editor-in-chief/the-more-you-knowabout-the-past-the-better-prepared-you-are-for-the-future/

Russo, M. A., Santarelli, D. M., & O'Rourke, D. (2017). The physiological effects of slow breathing in the healthy human. Breathe, 13(4), 298–309. https://doi.org/10.1183/20734735.009817

Schramme, T. (2023). Health as complete well-being: The WHO definition and beyond. Public Health Ethics, 16(3), 210–218. https://doi.org/10.1093/phe/ phad017

Segerstrom, S. C., & Miller, G. E. (2004). Psychological stress and the human immune system: A meta-analytic study of 30 years of inquiry. Psychological Bulletin, 130(4), 601–630. https://doi.org/10.1037/0033-2909.130.4.601

Sissons, C. (2020, May 27). What is the average percentage of water in the human body? Medical News Today. https://www.medicalnewstoday.com/articles/ what-percentage-of-the-human-body-is-water

Soliva-Estruch, M., Tamashiro, K. L., & Daskalakis, N. P. (2023). Genetics and epigenetics of stress: New avenues for an old concept. Neurobiology of Stress,

23, 100525. https://doi.org/10.1016/j.ynstr.2023.100525

SpinalCord.com Team. (2021, April 26). What you need to know about brain oxygen deprivation. SpinalCord.com. https://www.spinalcord.com/blog/whathappens-after-a-lack-of-oxygen-to-the-brain

Spitzer, C., Koch, B., Grabe, H. J., Ewert, R., Barnow, S., Felix, S. B., Ittermann, T., Obst, A., Völzke, H., Gläser, S., & Schäper, C. (2011). Association of airflow limitation with trauma exposure and post-traumatic stress disorder. European Respiratory Journal, 37(5), 1068–1075. https://doi. org/10.1183/09031936.00028010

Stolkiner, J. (1997). The emotional functioning of the breath and it's applications in therapy. Energy & Consciousness, International Journal of Core Energetics, 5, 59–77. https://www.coreenergetics.org/wp-content/uploads/2015/11/6Stolkiner-J.-The-Emotional-Functioning-of-the-Breath-and-Its-Applications-in-Therapy.-EC-5.1-1997.pdf

Streeter, C. C., Gerbarg, P. L., Brown, R. P., Scott, T. M., Nielsen, G. H., Owen, L., Sakai, O., Sneider, J. T., Nyer, M. B., & Silveri, M. M. (2020). Thalamic gamma aminobutyric acid level changes in major depressive disorder after a 12-week Iyengar yoga and coherent breathing intervention. The Journal of Alternative and Complementary Medicine, 26(3), 190–197. https://doi. org/10.1089/acm.2019.0234

Tareen, Z. (2022, February 18). Eleusinian mysteries: The secret rites no one dared talk about. The Collector. https://www.thecollector.com/the-eleusinian-mysteries-ancient-greece/

Tukiri, C. H. (2023). Te Waihotia o Whakaotirangi: What Whakaotirangi left behind. [Master's thesis, The University of Auckland] The University of Auckland ResearchSpace. https://researchspace.auckland.ac.nz/handle/2292/68099

Walters, P. (2023, July 26). What is transformational breathing? [Explained]. Eye Mind Spirit. https://www.eyemindspirit. com/post/transformational-breath-for-healing

Watson, K. (2019, June 11). Is rebirthing therapy safe and effective? Healthline. https://www.healthline.com/ health/rebirthing

White, G. (2024, August 14). Breathing to boost natural immunity. Buteyko Breathing Clinics. https://www. buteykobreathing.nz/blog/breathing-to-boost-natural-immunity

Winfrey, O. (n.d). Quote. In Vallejo, M. (2023, December 11). 60 best stress quotes for inner calm. Mental Health Center Kids. https://mentalhealthcenterkids. com/blogs/ articles/quotes-about-stress

World Health Organization. (2020). Who guidelines on physical activityandsedentarybehaviourataglance.https://iris.who. int/bitstream/handle/10665/337001/9789240014886-eng.pdf

Yousif, M. E. (2016). The double slit experiment—explained. Journal of Physical Mathematics, 7(2), 1–10. https://doi. org/10.4172/2090-0902.1000179

Zhang, Y., Chen, S., Zhang, Z., Duan, W., Zhao, L., Weinschenk, G., Luh, W.-M., Anderson, A. K., & Dai, W. (2023). Effect of meditation on brain activity during an attention task: A comparison study of ASL and BOLD task MRI. Brain Sciences, 13(12), 1653. https://doi.org/10.3390/ brainsci13121653

Image References

Adderley, C. (2023). Photo a Man and Woman Doing Martial Arts. In Pexel. https://www.pexels.com/search/karate/

Chirova, B. (2024). All chapter first pages display pictures. [AI-generated image]. DALL·E.

Green, A. (2020). Black psychologist with african american client [Image]. In Pexels. https://www.pexels.com/photo/black-psychologist-with-african-american-client-5699424/

Kaboompics.com. (2020). Peaceful Lady Sitting in Padmasana Pose While Meditating on Mat [Image]. In Pexels. https://www.pexels.com/search/breath/

Karpovich, V. figure 9-2, (2021, July 19). An elderly couple meditating at the park [Image]. Pexels https://www.pexels.com/photo/an-elderly-couple-meditating-at-the-park-8940618/

OpenClipart-Vectors. (2013). Anatomy-lungs-breathing-human [Image]. In Pixabay. https://pixabay.com/vectors/anatomy-lungs-breathing-human-145696/

Patricia Eschuk, Fine Artist, figure 7-1 (2024/09/23) Creator-Dreamer

Patricia Eschuk, Fine Artist, figure 7-2 (2024/08/15/09/23) Communicator-Orator

Patricia Eschuk, Fine Artist, figure 7-3 (2024/09/23) Integrator-Solidifier

Patricia Eschuk, Fine Artist, figure 7-4 (2024/09/23) Inspirer-Passionate

Patricia Eschuk, Fine Artist, figure 7-5 (2024/09/23) Manifestor/Achiever

Pires, R. (2018). Red Lantern Lamp Turned on. In Pexel. https://www.pexels.com/search/light/

RDNE Stock project. Figure 9-3, (2021b, June 2). People standing on green grass field [Image]. Pexels https://www.pexels.com/photo/people-standing-on-greengrass-field-8172931/

Shkraba, A. (2020). People meditating in a yoga class [Image]. In Pexels. https://www.pexels.com/photo/people-meditating-in-a-yoga-class-5890296/

Strauss, D.E. (2024). Heart and rose logo mark. [AI-generated image]. Donna Evans Strauss

Strauss Evans, Donna, Blessings From a Thousand Generations, figure 5-2, (Balboa Press 2011, ISBN:978-1-4525-3192-2

Tomášková, I. (2024). Man Thoughts Idea. In Pixabay. https://pixabay.com/illustrations/ai-generated-man-thoughts-idea-8621048/

Wei, W. (2019). Photo of night sky full of stars. In Pexels. https://www.pexels.com/photo/photo-of-night-sky-full-of-stars-2753432/

© [kinara art design] /Adobe Stock. figure 1-1, Generated with AI, https://stock. adobe.com/images/a-profile-of-a-girl-exhaling-a-colorful-stream-of-stars-and-cosmic-elements/946147240/ 946813405-combined

© [InnerPeace] /Adobe Stock. figure 2-1, https://stock.adobe.com/images/painted-wall-relief-depicting-tutankhamun-and-his-soul-ka-embracing-osiris-and-goddess-nut-inside-the-famous-tomb-of-tutankhamun-kv62-found-by-howard-carterin-1922-in-the-valley-of-kings-luxor-egypt/812496192

© [Irina Ukrainets] /Adobe Stock. figure 2-2, Generated with AI, https://stock. adobe.com/images/cosmic-birth-concept-ai-generated-image-baby-floating-in-colorful-galaxy-with-stars-and-particles-child-in-space-represents-new-life-creationand-imagination-sci-fi-digital-art-ai/879623299

Visit DonnaEvansStrauss.com
to learn more about Donna,
including her books, programs and meditations.

www.ingramcontent.com/pod-product-compliance
Lightning Source LLC
Chambersburg PA
CBHW051145120626
46547CB00012B/948